W9-DAN-594

# INDIANS OF
# NORTH AMERICA

# INDIANS OF NORTH AMERICA

A REFERENCE
FIRST BOOK

**DANIEL JACOBSON**

FRANKLIN WATTS
NEW YORK | LONDON | TORONTO
SYDNEY | 1983

Cover photographs courtesy of:
Ginger Giles: center; Franklin Watts: lower right;
Library of Congress: upper right;
Smithsonian Institution National Anthropological Archives,
Bureau of American Ethnology Collection: upper left, lower left;
Museum of the American Indian, Heye Foundation: bottom.


Photographs courtesy of
American Museum of Natural History: pp. 3 (Rota),
14, 50 (Rodman Wanamaker);
The New York Public Library Picture Collection:
pp. 11, 18, 33, 64, 68, 69, 70;
Smithsonian Office of Anthropology,
Bureau of American Ethnology Collection:
pp. 22, 29, 33, 63, 72, 88;
Library of Congress: pp. 30, 57, 73;
Museum of the American Indian, Heye Foundation:
pp. 6, 24, 39, 76, 78; Ron Greenberg: p. 44;
Union Pacific Railroad: pp. 49, 81;
The Public Archives of Canada: p. 77;
Woolaroc Museum: p. 79.


Map on p. 20 reprinted with permission of
Hammond, Inc., Maplewood, N.J.
Map on p. 26 from *The New Book of Knowledge,*
Volume 9, published by Grolier.


Library of Congress Cataloging in Publication Data

Jacobson, Daniel, 1923-
Indians of North America

(A Reference first book)
Summary: A lexicon of terms relating to the North
American Indian. Includes Apache, Bureau of Indian
s, hogan, Maya, Pocahontas, and Trail of Tears.
1. Indians of North America—Dictionaries,
Juvenile. [1. Indians of North America—
Dictionaries] I. Title. II. Series.
983     970.004′97′00321     83-5757.
ISBN 0-531-04647-8

Dedicated to the fond memory of Ency Abbott
and Kinney Williams, Coushatta of Bayou Blue.
Both are now with the Master of Life.
May they rest in peace.

# INDIANS OF
# NORTH AMERICA

**AMERICAN INDIAN MOVEMENT (AIM).** The American Indian Movement (AIM) was founded in Minneapolis in 1966 by Chippewa led by Dennis Banks and Clyde Bellecourt who hoped to force government agencies to improve services to the Indian community. AIM's image—militant and tough—is derived, however, from the old warrior societies of the Teton Sioux. Dennis Banks and Russell Means, another AIM leader, are concerned about greater equality and the civil rights of Indian people. They are disturbed by depressed living conditions on the reservations, by high infant mortality and low life expectancy, and by the high rates of unemployment and suicide.

In 1972 AIM helped to raid and occupy the Bureau of Indian Affairs (BIA) offices in Washington, D.C. In 1973 they seized the village of Wounded Knee on the Pine Ridge Reservation in South Dakota. For seventy-one days they withstood the threat of a besieging force of United States marshals, FBI agents, and BIA police. Two Indians were killed, and one FBI agent was wounded. Russell Means and Dennis Banks were jailed.

TV, newspaper, and magazine coverage of the modern day confrontation at Wounded Knee was extensive. The plight of the American Indian became well known to the average American. And AIM goes on. *See also* BUREAU OF INDIAN AFFAIRS.

**APACHE.** The Athapascan-speaking Apache arrived in the Southwest from the far north early in the sixteenth century. The Kiowa Apache and the Lipan made their homes on the Plains; the Jicarilla in north-central New Mexico and neighboring Colorado; the Mescalero in the Pecos River drainage; and much farther west, the Chiricahua in the Mexico–Arizona–New Mexico border country; and the Western Apache in east-central Arizona.

Apache on and near the Plains often hunted the bison. Those farther west, though hunters too, were primarily gatherers. They gathered mescal, the staple in the diet, as well as piñon nuts, acorns, screw beans, a wide variety of seeds and berries, and the fruits of the cacti. They also planted crops such as maize, squash, and beans. What they could not eat they stored in hillside caves.

The Apache were fighters and raiders. They fought the Spaniards, the Pueblo peoples, the Comanche, and the Ute. They won important victories and they suffered humiliating defeats. But their greatest challenge, survival, came with the arrival of the Americans in the nineteenth century.

When Americans moved into Apache country, the Apache retaliated. They hit and ran. Their small bands attacked stagecoaches, freight caravans, and ranches. The United States government ordered the Apaches to move to four reservations, three in Arizona Territory and one in New Mexico Territory. General George Crook and his soldiers urged the Apache to comply with the government order. Many did, but some did not. Victorio, an Apache, continued the raids on the American settlements. He kept two thousand American troops at bay from 1874 to 1880, until he was killed in Mexico. Nana and Geronimo, his successors, took over. Geronimo did not surrender until 1886.

The Apache were filled with despair. Poverty, disease, and bitterness were rife. Against their will, the former warriors and raiders began to farm their reservation lands. In 1934, as a result of the Indian Reorganization Act, the small Apache bands were organized into tribes—the White Mountain Apache Tribe, the San Carlos Apache Tribe, and the Mescalero Apache Tribe. They began to work on and off the reservations, in mines and on ranches and farms.

The Apache began to move into the twentieth century. In 1954 the White Mountain Recreational Enterprise was formed. The Western Apache began to use their timber resources. On the San Carlos Reservation, a profitable ranching industry of Hereford cattle was created. A tribal farm, with grain, cotton, and alfalfa was begun. The Mescalero moved into tourism. In 1975 they opened a 134-room deluxe resort called the Inn of the Mountain Gods. On the property are an artificial lake, swimming pools, tennis courts, and a golf course. At Dulce Lake the Jicarilla, too, built a fine motel.

On and off the reservations the Apache are working today as mechanics, plumbers, carpenters, nurses, secretaries, and laborers. They are attending schools and colleges. The tribal councils are active. An Apache Nations Alliance has been created. Its aims are to protect Apache resources and to keep Apache culture alive. The Apache number over fifteen thousand. *See also* GERONIMO and THE INDIAN REORGANIZATION ACT.

**AZTECS.** The great god Huitzilopochtli, the Hummingbird, is said to have counseled the Aztecs to move into the Valley of Mexico. They arrived early in the thirteenth century. By 1248 they were encamped on the western shore of Lake Texcoco. They learned from their neighbors that Quetzalcoatl, the local god of peace, was visiting distant shores and that he would return one day to reclaim his valley. The tale was one that the Aztecs would long remember. They talked of wars and conquest; they talked about building a great city. In 1325 they started work on Tenochtitlán (today Mexico City), soon to become the Aztec capital.

**A reconstruction of the Aztec temple at Tenochtitlán**

Aztec power grew. They thrashed their sister cities in the valley in battle and brought many captives to Tenochtitlán. Human sacrifices, in which hearts were torn from the victims' bodies, were made to Huitzilopochtli. The Aztecs pushed to both coasts and south to Guatemala. Their traders, the *pochteca*, shipped rope, cloth, and tools to the distant south. Cacao, rubber, cotton, birds' feathers, and even emeralds from Colombia arrived in exchange. Tenochtitlán was becoming wealthy. It had 250,000 people. Its warehouses bulged with goods. To Huitzilopochtli had been sacrificed many human hearts.

In Tenochtitlán there were rumors about Quetzalcoatl's return. Was he on the strange craft newly arrived on the Gulf of Mexico coast? No one knew for certain. On November 8, 1519, however, Hernando Cortes and his Spaniards moved into the Capital. Montezuma II, the Aztec leader, did little to stop them. But when the Spaniards ripped the idol of the Hummingbird from his perch in the great temple, the Aztecs stormed into battle. They drove the Spaniards from the city. Montezuma II was killed, some say by his own people, and some say by the Spaniards. Not until August 13, 1521, did the Spaniards finally capture the blood-soaked Aztec capital.

After the fall of Tenochtitlán, smallpox, typhus, and measles gripped the city. Death loomed everywhere. Warfare and disease had taken their toll. The Aztecs—century-long masters of the Valley of Mexico—could not recover. Most of their remaining numbers, in time, became peasants, farmers of the Mexican earth.

**BERING LAND BRIDGE.** There were times during the Ice Age when sea level dropped considerably, and land normally under water was exposed. The Asian and North American land masses were joined by the Bering land bridge—1,200 or more miles (1,931 km) broad—over which both mammals and humans could move easily.

The Bering land bridge was exposed between 55,000 and 45,000 years ago. It was also exposed 40,000 years ago, 30,000 years ago, and between 20,000 and 12,000 years ago. During any of these periods, or possibly in an earlier one, the first of the Indians, perhaps following land mammals such as woolly mammoth, mastodon, old bison, and musk ox moved over the land bridge from Asia to North America.

Best evidence today indicates that the migration was an early one. A caribou bone flesher, made by a human being and found at Old Crow Flats in the Yukon River drainage, has been dated at 27,000 years of age. The Indians, therefore, may have arrived in the New World 30,000 or 40,000 years ago or even earlier.

**BLACK HAWK** (1767–1838). A Sauk warrior and chief who attempted to stop the westward movement of American settlers. Schooled in warfare from youth, Black Hawk had already taken his first scalp at fifteen. He joined the British

**Black
Hawk**

during the War of 1812. He fought the Kentuckians on the River Raisin in Michigan and campaigned in Canada, Ohio, and Indiana.

Meanwhile, many of the Sauk and Fox had moved to lands west of the Mississippi. Those who remained at Saukenuk, near the mouth of Rock River, Illinois, had elected a new chief, Keokuk, an advocate of peace and an opponent of Black Hawk's. By 1814 the British and Americans were fighting near Saukenuk. Major Zachary Taylor, sent north to destroy the Sauk villages, was forced to withdraw. Black Hawk had played a leading role in the British-Indian victory.

In 1816 Keokuk and a reluctant Black Hawk went to St. Louis to sign the treaty by which the Sauk gave up their lands in the Illinois country. Keokuk moved his band west; Black Hawk was furious and refused to move.

Americans, sons of New England and New York moving through Ohio and Indiana, pushed into the Illinois country. Black Hawk decided to fight. Governor Reynolds of Illinois called out the militia. Federal troops assisted. They swept into Saukenuk and destroyed the village by fire on June 25, 1831. But Black Hawk and his people had slipped out and crossed the Mississippi River.

The following spring Black Hawk and his followers—two thousand warriors, men, women, and children—recrossed the Mississippi. Once more state and federal troops were called into drive out the Sauk. Keokuk, siding with the Americans, agreed to help.

In the so-called Black Hawk War, Black Hawk led his people north into Wisconsin. He sustained heavy losses. At the mouth of Bad Axe River, the Americans fell on the Sauk. Nearly three hundred were killed. Black Hawk himself escaped to the north but was captured and imprisoned in St. Louis.

Later freed, Black Hawk and his old enemy Keokuk toured the cities of the east. He dictated *The Autobiography of Black Hawk* in 1833. On October 3, 1838, the old warrior died near Iowaville, Iowa, on the Des Moines River.

**BUREAU OF INDIAN AFFAIRS (BIA)**. Created on March 11, 1824. On July 9, 1832, a bill was passed to appoint a Commissioner of Indian Affairs. He would supervise the BIA, serve under the Secretary of War, and manage all Indian affairs and relations. Newly elected President Andrew Jackson appointed Elbert Herring first commissioner. In 1849 BIA was transferred to the Department of the Interior, where it remains to this day.

BIA has three main functions: to protect the resources of the Indians (reservations, land, and minerals), to carry out federal programs authorized by Congress (often related to buildings, roads, wells, irrigation channels, and schools), and to create an environment in which the Indians can develop to their full potential on their own.

BIA has been harshly criticized. Indians complain that BIA has often been governed with a spirit hostile to the Indians. There is room for improvement in Indian education and housing, and especially, as the Indians see it, in the political decision-making process.

On November 2, 1972, American Indians marched on the BIA offices in Washington, D.C., along the so-called Trail of Broken Treaties. They were joined by members of the American Indian Movement (AIM). Protesting the government's failure to live up to past treaties, and the inability of BIA to find solutions to Indian problems, the marchers "invaded" the BIA building. They did not leave until November 8. A million dollars worth of damage was done, and many Indian records, documents, artifacts, and paintings were lost. *See also* AMERICAN INDIAN MOVEMENT (AIM).

**CALUMET.** The calumet, or peace pipe, was made of two shafts of reed or wood 2, 3, or even 4 feet (60, 90, or 120 cm) long. One shaft stood for the power of the male, the other for the fertility of the female. In short, the calumet was a symbol for life itself. It was often painted in various colors and decorated with the heads, tails, wings, and feathers of birds. When a tobacco bowl was added, the calumet became a sacred pipe; its smoke was offered to the gods.

The calumet was carried by ambassadors and travelers as a passport. It was used in ceremonies to bring favorable weather or rain. It was used to insure that agreements made between tribes and other peoples would not be violated. Singing and dancing were often parts of a calumet ceremony.

The Pawnee believed that the calumet was a gift from the sun. When the calumet was offered and accepted and when smoke was blown to the gods, any agreement made between the parties could not be broken.

**CAMP CIRCLE.** The first summer camping ground of a number of the Great Plains tribes. From their spring homes the various clans would move to a given location on the circle. The circle itself was made up of tepees three and four deep, with the east side open. The Crow camp circle might have as many as thirty-five hundred people camped within it. From the camp circle they moved to pursue bison.

**CHEROKEE.** The Iroquois-speaking Cherokee were farmers of the American Southeast in what is now North Carolina, Georgia, and Tennessee. They lived in towns and villages dominated by the seven-sided, dome-shaped council house, chunkey yard, and public granary. Nearby were the rectangular gable-roofed houses and the planted fields of maize, squash, beans, and tobacco. The women were the farmers and gatherers; the men, skillful in the use of bow and blowgun, were the hunters and fishermen.

Early in the eighteenth century the Cherokee numbered nearly twenty thousand; they lived in sixty-four towns and villages. In the severe fighting of the Revolutionary War, in which the Cherokee sided with the English, fifty Cherokee towns and villages were destroyed. To survive, the Cherokee fled to the mountains. Later they returned to found new towns, but there was no real peace until 1794. By that time hundreds of Cherokee had headed west. By 1819 several thousand had migrated.

In 1820 the Cherokee Nation, modeled after the government of the United States, was formed. In 1821 Sequoya introduced the Cherokee to the "talking leaves," an alphabet for the Cherokee language. By 1828 *The Cherokee Phoenix* was being printed in both Cherokee and English. Meanwhile the Georgia planters who had moved into Cherokee country wanted the Cherokee to leave. The Treaty of New Echota (1835), signed by one Cherokee faction, called for the Cherokee to move west. They were rounded up by the military and moved to Indian Territory (now Oklahoma). More than four thousand died on the bitter journey. For the Cherokee it was a "Trail of Tears."

More than a thousand Cherokee hid from the military in the mountains of western North Carolina. With the help of Col. William H. Thomas, land was purchased for them. They drafted a constitution and were soon known as the Eastern Band (1870). Towns and schools were built. In 1876 the Qualla Boundary or Reservation was established.

Many changes came in the 1900s: roads and cars, cash economy, cooperatives, the tourist industry, a United States Public Health Service hospital, and a nursing facility. By the 1950s only 10 percent of the eastern Cherokee were supported by farming; by the 1970s not one single family was engaged in farming. The Eastern Band numbers more than six thousand. In the west the Cherokee were granted allotments of land. They helped achieve statehood for Oklahoma in 1907 and have been active in their state's affairs ever since. Today they number more than fourteen thousand. *See also* JOHN ROSS; SEQUOYA; *and* TRAIL OF TEARS.

**Chief Joseph**

**CHIEF JOSEPH** (1832–1904). Chief Joseph of the Nez Percé tribe grew to manhood in the beautiful Wallowa Valley of northeastern Oregon. In the 1850s and 1860s white people began to settle in the valley. The Nez Percé at Lapwai (Idaho) signed the Treaty of 1863, but Joseph's band and others did not sign. It was expected that the Nez Percé would move to the reservation, but they did not.

In 1873 the lower Wallowa was set aside as an Indian reserve. Joseph was not satisfied. He asked for the return of all his beloved land and the removal of the white settlers. By 1875, however, the whites were homesteading in the valley once more. The nontreaty Nez Percé were ready for war.

They decided to fight and run. Under chiefs Looking Glass, White Bird, and Toohoolhoolzote they moved east over the Lolo Trail, with General O.O. Howard in hot pursuit. Joseph and the Wallowa band were among the fighters. The Nez Percé crossed the Bitterroot Range and moved south into Yellowstone National Park and north along the Clark Fork. Their aim was to flee to Canada—and freedom.

They did not make it. The Nez Percé were caught at the Bear Paws in Montana. Looking Glass and Toohoolhoolzote were already dead. White Bird had escaped. The surrender to generals Howard and Nelson A. Miles was left to Chief Joseph in 1877. "Hear me my chiefs. I am tired; my heart is sick and sad. From where the sun now stands I will fight no more forever."

The Nez Percé were removed to Ft. Leavenworth, Kansas, and later to Indian Territory. In 1883, thirty-three women and children were permitted to return to Lapwai. Chief Joseph and his band, however, were sent to the Colville Reservation in Washington. The Nez Percé chief died there on September 21, 1904. *See also* NEZ PERCÉ.

**CHINOOK.** The great traders of the lower Columbia River Valley, they were the middlemen between the Northwest Coast and tribes ranging east to the Great Plains. At the Dalles fair on the Columbia in early summer, the Chinook bought animal skins, dried bison meat, sheep horn, tobacco, elk-skin armor, and European trade axes. In exchange they sold the much-prized dentalia (white shells known as *hiqua* on the Northwest Coast) and slaves (often purchased from the California tribes), perhaps their most important trade item. They also sold slaves and elk-skin armor to the Makah and through them to the Nootka of Vancouver Island, in exchange for dentalia and the sea-going Nootka canoe.

In 1788 John Meares, an English seaman, sailed into Willapa Bay; in 1792 the American Robert Gray guided his ship, *Columbia Rediviva*, over the Columbia River bar. Others followed. Meriwether Lewis and William Clark came over land in 1805; the "Boston Men," the men of John Jacob Astor's ship *Tonquin*, and the Englishmen of the Hudson's Bay Company came. Astoria was established on the south side of the Columbia River directly opposite Chief Comcomly's plank house village.

The type of trade carried on by the Chinook changed much with the coming of the Boston Men, for the Americans brought new items to the Columbia River—tea kettles, glass beads, brass armbands, cloth, knives, guns, and rum. In return the Chinook offered beaver skins and elk-skin armor. These the Boston Men traded to tribes farther north for the sea otter pelt, the dominant item in the profitable China trade. Most Boston Men and Englishmen had a high regard for the Chinook—especially the women—as traders and hagglers.

In the 1830s the Chinook were struck down by the "ague fever," the "Cold Sick,"—probably a form of influenza or malaria, which crippled the Indian villages. The Chinook population, estimated at more than seven hundred in Comcomly's day, fell to just more than a hundred in 1885. Furthermore, the Chinook had intermarried with European and American settlers as well as with their Indian neighbors. They were soon scattered over the Warm Springs, Yakima, and Grande Ronde reservations in Oregon and Washington. Only a remnant remained on Willapa Bay.

By the 1900s, it appeared to most that the Chinook had ceased to exist. But such was not the case. On August 8, 1951, the Chinook Nation filed suit against the United States government, claiming aboriginal title to the land on the lower Columbia River. Two years later the Chinook Indian Tribe was incorporated under the laws of the state of Washington. For their former lands the Chinook were awarded $75,000 by the Indian Claims Commission on November 4, 1971.

**CHIPEWYAN.** Caribou hunters of the Canadian subarctic. In summer they speared the caribou in rivers and lakes; in winter they drove them into corrals where kills were made with bows and arrows. They hunted the musk ox and moose. They were fine trappers, gatherers, and fishermen.

While man was the provider, woman was the worker. On her back she carried food, furs, and household goods across the barren grounds; she also dragged the heavy toboggans and sledges. She raised the children and did all of the household chores.

The world of the Chipewyan was invaded by the English in 1717. By 1733 the newcomers had begun to build a fort—Fort Prince of Wales—near present-day Churchill in northern Manitoba. Before long Chipewyan bands began to bring their furs to the fort. They exchanged them for food, clothing, brass kettles, and medicine.

One of the newcomers, Samuel Hearne of the Hudson Bay Company, guided by Matonabbee, a Chipewyan hunter, went north and discovered Coppermine River in 1771. Later, when the French destroyed the English fort, Matonabbee was so grieved he killed himself (1782). His six wives and four children all died in the northern snow in 1783. Diseases, particularly smallpox, took a terrible toll on the Chipewyan in succeeding years. By 1788 Chipewyan bands were carrying their furs to Fort Chipewyan on Lake Athabasca.

Life has changed much since. Hunting, fishing, and trapping are still done. But today most Chipewyan earn their living as wage laborers. Bannock (made of white flour and baking powder, mixed with water and fried) has become the chief food. At Snowdrift in the Northwest Territories the Chipewyan live in government-built houses that have electricity and heat.

**CHIPPEWA.** Also known as Ojibway, "people whose moccasins have puckered seams," the Chippewa were hunters, fishermen, gatherers, and sometimes farmers of the Upper Great Lakes. In the seventeenth and early eighteenth centuries they lived in the large villages of Sault Ste. Marie, Mackinac, L'Arbre Croche, Green Bay, and Chequamegon on Lakes Huron, Michigan, and Superior. Chippewa bands, in their birch bark–covered wigwams, could also be found at scattered locations north, south, and west of the lakes.

In the spring Chippewa tapped the maple trees, scooped up the sap, boiled it in vats, and stored the sugar in the *makuk,* or birch bark container. The men built canoes, toboggans, traps, and snowshoes; the women made a variety of nets, bags, mats, clothing, and musical instruments. It was the season of the initiation of members into the *Midewiwin,* or Grand Medicine Society—those who would be trained to cure the sick. Summer was devoted to fishing and to berry and bark collecting; south of the lakes green maize was harvested. At the rapids at Sault Ste. Marie a favorite activity was netting the whitefish. Autumn was the time for gathering wild rice and for hunting animals. It was also the time for the Feast of the Dead. Winter activities included trapping, hunting, and ice fishing.

**Chippewa Indian girls harvesting wild rice**

During these years the Chippewa pursued the precious beaver pelts and exchanged them for French trade goods. The Chippewa gradually drifted away from their villages. Chequamegon, once with more than a thousand people, was much reduced in size. The Chippewa battled the Sioux, and late in the eighteenth century occupied numerous lake and river sites in Wisconsin and Minnesota.

The British replaced the French in the Upper Great Lakes in the 1760s; by 1796 agents of the American Fur Company were operating trading posts in the Chippewa country. Other Americans came. They pushed into the mining areas and timber lands, and the Chippewa were forced, in ten treaties, to give up much of their land. They retained only the reservation lands in Michigan, Wisconsin, Minnesota, and North Dakota.

On the reservations in the twentieth century, unemployment, substandard housing, and inadequate medical care and schooling have been major problems. Many Chippewa, therefore, left the reservations for urban areas. They moved to Chicago, Milwaukee, Detroit, Cleveland, Minneapolis-St. Paul, and Duluth. The Chippewa found adjusting to city life difficult.

But much progress has been made in recent years on reservations and in cities alike. The Chippewa have taken matters into their own hands. The Ojibway Indian Trailer Park near Baraga, the Red Cliff Arts and Crafts Center, a campground and marina opened in 1975, the Lac du Flambeau Reservation Community Center, the tribal campground and marina and fish hatchery, the Radisson Inn on the Grand Portage Reservation, and the New Odanah Village all testify to a new Chippewa vitality. Housing and medical care have been improved. More Chippewa children are in the schools. There is a growing pride in the Chippewa heritage and in Chippewa identity. Today some thirty thousand Chippewa live in Minnesota alone, and nearly ten thousand in Minneapolis-St. Paul. More than fifty thousand Ojibway live in Canada; there are numerous bands in Ontario, Manitoba, and Saskatchewan.

**CLOTHING.** Varied from culture area to culture area. Men's clothing differed somewhat from women's.

Men on the Plains wore a tanned buckskin shirt to the knees, a breechcloth, leggings, and hide moccasins. The women wore a long shirt-dress with cape sleeves, a belt, leggings to the knees, and moccasins. In winter the bison robe was universal. With the coming of the Europeans much more decoration was added, especially in beaded designs. Also added was the tailed warbonnet with eagle feathers, worn by the warriors who had collected coups.

The Indians on the Northwest Coast wore little clothing. The men did wear cedar bark blankets or robes held in place by sealskin belts. They wore rain capes when necessary and hats woven of cedar bark or spruce root. In very cold weather nobles wore robes of fur. The women wore the cedar bark apron. Neither sex donned leggings or moccasins.

In the Southwest the children went about naked. The men wore breechcloth, rabbit-skin robe, and yucca-fiber sandals, and the women wore woven cotton dresses. At Taos, blankets, moccasins, and heelless shoes became important clothing items. The women garbed themselves in brightly colored shawls. In the nineteenth century there were marked influences from the Plains. Men wore buckskin shirts; women, deerskin dresses. Today the young at Taos prefer Anglo-style clothing, as do most Indians, generally, in the United States and Canada.

**COMANCHE.** The Comanche have been called "Lords of the South Plains." They had moved to the grasslands of Oklahoma and Texas from Colorado and the Great Basin early in the eighteenth century. They learned to use horses while hunting bison. They lived in tepees, and relied on pemmican (made from bison meat, berries, and fat) as a staple in their diet. They moved about the countryside in bands, sought visions, and gloried in warfare. They had become a typical Plains people.

But their reign as "lords" was relatively short. White settlers pushed into Comanche country and the bison began to disappear. The Comanche raided nearby communities, but it was all in vain. On April 25, 1868, the Comanche, like the Cheyenne, Arapaho, Kiowa, and Kiowa Apache, were assigned to a reservation. They were given farm tools and were expected to farm the land. Today many Comanche live in Oklahoma. *See also* QUANAH PARKER.

**COUSHATTA.** The Muskhogean-speaking Coushatta live today along Bayou Blue, near Elton, Louisiana, and on the Alabama-Coushatta reservation, near Livingston, Texas. They formerly lived in Alabama. Hernando de Soto, the Spanish explorer, found them near the Tennessee River in 1540. In the seventeenth century they joined other tribes in the Alabama River drainage and became members of the Creek Confederacy.

Like other Creek towns, the Coushatta town had its public square, its chunkey yard and hot house, and its clan-owned fields. The Coushatta women were the farmers and gatherers, and the men were the hunters and fishermen.

Hunting became increasingly important in the eighteenth century as the English and French traders moved into the Creek country.

The Coushatta were partial to the French. In 1717 the French built Fort Toulouse near the fork of the Coosa and Tallapoosa rivers, just north of the Coushatta town. There the Coushatta brought their deer, bear, bison, and otter pelts and exchanged them for blue and red limbourg (cloth), guns, bullets, powder, razors, needles, knives, ribbons, and woolen goods. The French were to remain at Fort Toulouse until 1763, when they were forced by the Treaty of Paris, signed with the British, to leave most of North America.

Many of the Coushatta left their "mother town" as well. Twenty families moved to Red River in Louisiana in 1795; others went to eastern Texas. In 1822 there were 350 Coushatta on Red River. By 1850 most were living near the Trinity, Neches, and Sabine rivers in Texas. A number were on the Calcasieu in Louisiana, where they founded Indian Village. But land purchases by whites forced the Coushatta to leave. In 1884 they made land purchases themselves on both sides of Bayou Blue.

On the bayou the Coushatta relied, for the most part, on hunting, fishing, and gathering for their livelihood. They had no public square, no chunkey yard, no hot house. They lived in small bark-roofed huts. In 1893 the Reverend Paul Leeds, a Congregationalist minister, arrived in the community. Under his direction the Coushatta built the St. Pateer's Congregational Church.

Early in the twentieth century when the French-Canadian and Midwestern farmers turned to rice as the great commercial crop of southwestern Louisiana, the Coushatta were hired as field hands. Behind their own modest dwellings they began to plant their own gardens. By 1950 the Coushatta numbered about 250.

In 1953 the Bureau of Indian Affairs withdrew its relatively meager services of schooling and medical aid to the Coushatta. These were not restored until 1973 when the Coushatta were recognized as a tribe by the Department of the Interior, due largely to the work of Ernest Sickey, Tribal Chairman.

The Coushatta are still relatively poor. Unemployment is high, about 50 percent. Yet a new community house has been built and new housing is going up. In 1977 an Overall Economic Development Program was announced. There is a new feeling of hope in the community.

The Coushatta number 350 on Bayou Blue today. There are a few Coushatta in Oklahoma, in Houston, and on the Alabama-Coushatta Reservation in Texas. *See also* CREEKS.

**CRADLE.** In North America, Indian babies were bound or supported in cradles or cradleboards during the first months of life. There were a few exceptions. Eskimo mothers carried their babies about in fur parkas. There were Athapascans who placed their babies in bags of moss, and in Mexico babies were carried on mothers' hips. Various forms of cradles were found everywhere else.

**An Iroquois woman with her baby in a cradleboard**

The Algonquian tribes of northeastern North America carved a thin, rectangular wooden board with a projecting foot rest, which they painted and decorated. After being swaddled, the baby was tied to the board with a rope.

On the northwest coast the baby was put in a dugout cradle, a small box made of cedar. In the far north a single piece of birch or other bark was used. The bed was of fur, and the baby was lashed to it with babiche. The bison hunters made skin cradles, and in the Great Basin, cradles were made using basketry techniques.

The Paiute made a cradleboard of unpeeled willows, called a "boat cradle," for the newborn and a cradleboard for older babies. The larger cradleboard was made over a chokecherry frame. A willow platform was added, and the frame was covered with buckskin. Added, too, were a hood, a foot strap, and a beadwork design. The Paiute mother carried a baby on her back with the support of a tumpline.

**CREEKS.** Hunters and farmers of the American Southeast. Their clan-owned lands lined the river valleys of Alabama and Georgia. In the eighteenth century they lived in some fifty towns and villages. A public square was at the town's center. Nearby were the chunkey yard, where the Creeks played their ball games in summer, and the hot house, where they played in winter. The Creeks built their own homes just beyond the public square.

The eighteenth century brought the French and English traders to the Creek towns. In the nineteenth century came the land-hungry Americans. At Horseshoe Bend, March 27, 1814, Andrew Jackson defeated the Creeks in battle, and the clan-owned lands were lost. The Creeks were forced to give up all of their land east of the Mississippi River in 1832. Between 1836 and 1840, they were forced to move to Indian Territory in Oklahoma.

But the Creek spirit could not be crushed. They formed the Creek Nation in 1839. It lasted until 1907 when Oklahoma became a state. More than thirteen thousand Creeks still live in Oklahoma. *See also* COUSHATTA; *and* ALEXANDER MCGILLIVRAY.

**CROW.** Originally farmers near the western Great Lakes, the Crow became bison hunters on the Great Plains in the eighteenth and nineteenth centuries. They built tepees, used dog and horse travois, ate pemmican on their travels, and waged war on their Sioux and Blackfoot enemies. Young men sought visions and participated in the Sun Dance.

ARCTIC OCEAN

HUDSON BAY

Eskimo

A R C T I C

Eskimo

Eskimo

Eskimo

Ahtena

Hare

Dogrib

Yellowknife

CANADIAN

Tlingit

NORTHWEST

Haida

Tsimshian

Beaver

Chipewyan

Sarsi

SUB - ARCTIC

Naskapi

Montagnais

Beothuk

COAST

Sabish

Blood

Assiniboin

Cree

Algonkin

Micmac

Nootka

Kutenai

WESTERN
PLATEAU

Blackfeet

Chippewa

Ottawa

Abnaki

Chinook

Nez
Percé

PLAINS

Mandan

Huron

Massachuset

PACIFIC

Palute

Crow

Dakota

Fox

NORTHEAST

Iroquois

GREAT

Shoshone

(Sioux)

Erie

Lenni-
Lenape

Pomo

Ute

AND

Illinois

Miami

CALIFORNIA

BASIN

Cheyenne

Omaha

Powhatan

Salinan

Paiute

Arapaho

Osage

Shawnee

Tuscarora

ATLANTIC OCEAN

Yokut

Kiowa

PRAIRIES

Cherokee

Hopi

Navajo

Wichita

Chickasaw

Creek

OCEAN

Zuni

Pueblos

SOUTHWEST DESERT

Commanche

Caddo

SOUTHEAST

Koasati

Seminole

Seri

Apache

Concho

Yaqui

NORTHERN

Lagunero

Coahuiltec

GULF OF
MEXICO

Arawak

MEXICO

Antilles

CARIBBEAN
SEA

NORTH AMERICAN
INDIANS

Toltec

Tarascan

Aztec

Maya

Mixtec

MESOAMERICA

Zapotec

Culture Areas   ●   Major Tribes

Miles

0   200   400   600   800

In summer the Crow met in camp circle. Then, mounted on horseback and armed with bows and arrows or guns, they rode around the bison herds. After the kills, Crow women stripped the skin from the bison, cut the meat in thin slivers, and hung them on racks to dry. They prepared the pemmican and stored it in rawhide containers called *parfleches.*

On May 7, 1868, the Crow signed the Fort Laramie Treaty, accepting the reservation as life changed all around them. The bison disappeared; their warrior days were over. In 1904 the Department of the Interior banned the Sun Dance. White men began to lease land on the Crow Reservation.

In 1942 there were 2,100 Crow living on the reservation; by 1969 there were more than 3,500. There is good low-sulphur coal on the reservation, and some of it is being mined today. But the Crow Tribal Council opposes giving long leases to the big coal companies.

**CULTURE AREAS** Geographical regions where the ecological base and culture are similar. Food, clothing, housing, language, manufactures, religion, and political and social organization are among the traits that determine the culture areas. On the Northwest Coast, for example, the people lived in villages, and the housetype was rectangular and made of wooden planks; salmon was the staple food; manufactures included fine canoes and wooden boxes; art—woodworking, metalworking, painting, and sculpture—was an important value; there were winter ceremonials including the *potlatch*; and there were social classes—nobles, commoners, and slaves. All of the tribes on the Northwest Coast did not conform strictly to the above pattern, but they were similar. Certainly no other culture area in North America was quite the same. *See also* POTLATCH.

Daniel Jacobson's map on page 20, *North American Indians,* includes thirteen culture areas: Arctic (Eskimo), Canadian Subarctic, Northwest Coast, Western Plateau, Great Basin, California, Plains and Prairies, Northeast, Southeast, Southwest Desert, Northern Mexico, Mesoamerica, and Antilles.

# E-F

**EARTH LODGE.** The semisubterranean circular home of the Pawnee, Arikara, Omaha, Ponca, and Osage. After removing the earth from a large circle, 50 feet (15 m) in diameter and 2 to 4 feet (60 to 120 cm) deep, Pawnee men

An earth lodge

erected wooden posts within the circle. Beams were then laid in the crotches of the posts. Other posts were laid against the beams. In the center, long posts and beams were added to support the roof. An opening was left for the smoke from the fireplace to escape. Willow branches were tied securely over the entire frame, except for the open front on the east. Pawnee women added a heavy thatch of dried grass, topped by shingles of sod and earth. The long entranceway was made in the same way.

A number of families might live in the earth lodge. They were separated by mats suspended from the beams. Platform beds were set up on the sides. At the rear stood an altar, and on the west wall a sacred bundle wrapped in deerskin.

A large Pawnee community could boast as many as 180 earth lodges and a population of 3,500.

**CHARLES EDENSAW** (1835–1920). The finest of the artists among the Haida of the Queen Charlotte Islands. He was born at Cape Ball, Graham Island, but grew up at Skidegate and later moved to Masset. Under the watchful eye of an uncle, Albert Edward Edensaw, he perfected his talents. He worked in wood, silver, and gold. He made fine drawings and sketches. He was a keen crafts-man in argillite (carbonaceous shale), a material found in the Queen Charlotte Islands. A variety of pipes, plates, model totem poles, and replicas of storage boxes, now exhibited in museums, attest to Edensaw's extraordinary ability.

The Haida artist had high hopes that his son, Gyinawen, would follow him in the arts and carry on the Haida tradition. But the young man drowned at Rivers Inlet when he was eighteen. Charles Edensaw's grief knew no bounds.

In 1910 the artist was stricken with tuberculosis. He lived on in relative obscurity at Masset and died there in 1920.

But Edensaw's art—Haida art—has certainly not died. It has been revived in recent years. One of the current Haida artists is William R. Reid, a great grand-nephew of Charles Edensaw. *See also* HAIDA.

**ESKIMO.** The Eskimo live in perhaps the harshest of North American environ-ments. There are Eskimo in Alaska, the Canadian Arctic, Labrador, and Greenland. In the Canadian Arctic, for example, summers are short and cool, the subsoil is permanently frozen, and plant life is limited to dwarf willows, lichens, mosses, and sedges. The winters are bitter cold; the land lies in dark-ness for three to four months. Yet the caribou move north onto the tundra in summer and from time immemorial the seal, walrus, and whale have inhabited the Arctic seas.

In summer, using the *kayak,* or skin canoe propelled by a double bladed paddle, and making thrusts with the harpoon, the Eskimo made sea mammal kills. Meat, blubber, and light skins were provided by the ringed seal; meat, blubber, and hides for kayak covers and ivory for implements were provided by the walrus, and baleen and oil were provided by the whale. Summer was also the season for making caribou kills. Caribou skins were used for clothing; the sinew for thread; the blood, fat, marrow, and meat for food; and the antlers for bows. Summer was also a season for fishing and snaring or trapping small game.

**An Eskimo family in front
of igloo made of skins**

Canadian Arctic Eskimos often ate their meat raw. Much of the food taken in summer was stored for winter use. Caches were made on rock piles, under beach rocks, and in caves or trenches beyond the reach of dogs and other animals.

In winter there was *maupok* hunting, or waiting for the seal at the breathing hole. There was also ice fishing in which both men and women participated.

The Eskimo of the Canadian Arctic were builders of the igloo, or snow-block house. In the summer they lived in the skin tent. They wore tailored clothing made of animal skins and furs. They developed snow goggles and learned to use the sledge and dog team. In short, they learned over time to adjust to the Canadian Arctic environment.

Adaptations made by the Eskimo in other areas were different, of course. In southwestern Alaska, life revolved around salmon rather than sea mammals, and raw meat was rarely eaten. The igloo was unknown. The Caribou Eskimo were specialized caribou hunters. In Greenland, life more or less paralleled life in the Canadian Arctic.

But traditional Eskimo culture has been much affected by European, American, and Canadian contacts. The Norsemen were on Greenland's east coast in A.D. 980. The Russians appeared in Alaskan waters in the eighteenth century, and in 1840 an Englishman established a shore-based whaling station in the Canadian Arctic. Trading posts, missionaries, and the Royal Canadian Mounted Police followed.

At remote Pelly Bay in the Canadian Arctic, changes came very late. A Roman Catholic missionary did not arrive until 1935; a government school was constructed in 1962. Father Henry performed the religious duties, provided medical care, taught the Eskimos Canadian law, and ran the trading store.

In 1967 the Eskimo at Pelly Bay still lived in igloos in winter and tents in summer. Since then many new modern homes have been built. A nursing station, a fish processing plant, and a full-fledged cooperative have been established. The co-op purchased an airplane, a DC 4, in 1971 to deliver the co-op's products to market. There is even talk of tourism at Pelly Bay. The traditional culture has all but ceased. The Canadian Arctic Eskimo, as well as Eskimo everywhere, have arrived in the twentieth century.

**FIVE CIVILIZED TRIBES.** The Cherokee, Chickasaw, Choctaw, Creek, and Seminole, who were removed from their ancestral lands in the Southeast and forced to migrate to Indian Territory, were known collectively as the Five Civilized Tribes.

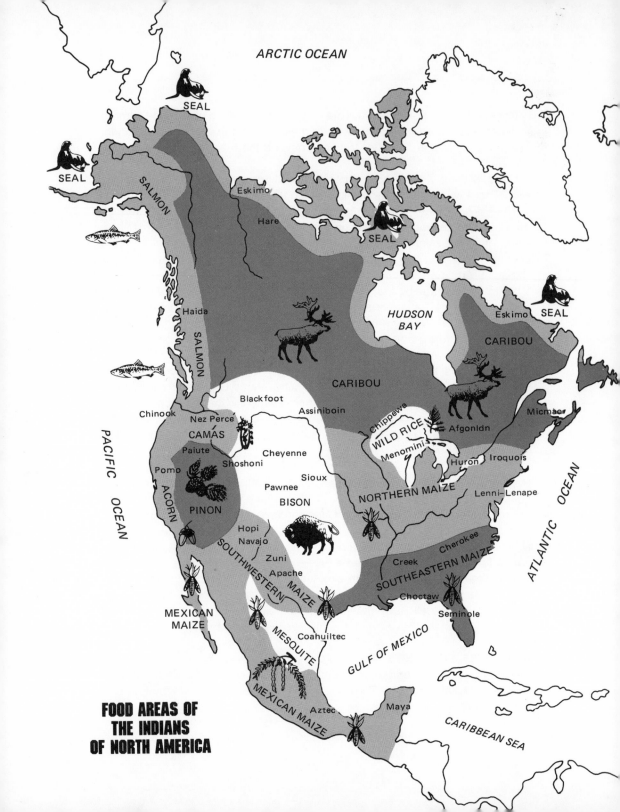

FOOD AREAS OF
THE INDIANS
OF NORTH AMERICA

**FOOD AREAS.** The anthropologist, Clark Wissler realized that humans often specialize in their eating habits. One food may well become a staple in their diet. He devised a map of the *Food Areas of the New World* to show the Indian staples. In North America, including the Caribbean, he found two hunting areas (Caribou Area and Bison Area), one fishing area (Salmon Area), one gathering area (Wild Seeds), and two farming areas (Area of Intensive Agriculture and Manioc Area).

Others have modified Dr. Wissler's map. Daniel Jacobson, in his *Food Areas of the Indians of North America* on page 26, includes three hunting areas (Seal, Caribou, and Bison), one fishing area (Salmon), five gathering areas (Acorn, Camas, Piñon, Mesquite, and Wild Rice), and four farming areas (Northern Maize, Southeastern Maize, Southwestern Maize, and Mexican Maize).

**GERONIMO** (1829–1909). A leading warrior and war chief of the Chiricahua Apache. Son of a Nednis Apache from Mexico and an Apache-Mexican woman from the headwaters of the Gila River in New Mexico, Geronimo spent his boyhood in his mother's home territory. There he learned to hunt, ride, wrestle, and to use the bow and arrow, lance, and gun. There he learned that treachery was often more prized than bravery. On trips to his father's people he learned about the mountains and deserts of the wider Apache country.

As a young man Geronimo lost his mother, wife, and children in a Mexican raid. Their deaths caused him to hate the Mexicans. He served under the great Apache leaders, Cochise and Mangas Coloradas, and he led raiding parties into Mexico. When the Americans entered the Apacheria, Geronimo and the Apache turned on them as well. They attacked wagon trains, ranches, and mines. They hit and ran. Americans were forced to seek refuge in larger communities.

In 1883 General George Crook was sent to Arizona to deal with the growing Apache menace. At a meeting with Geronimo in the Sierra Madre in Mexico, the general urged the Apache leader to move his people to the San Carlos Reservation. Geronimo did, but reservation life was hardly to his liking. In 1885 he and his band fled south to Mexico and began raiding once more. The American settlements in Arizona and New Mexico panicked. Crook pursued

Geronimo

the Apache leader, but Geronimo did not surrender until 1887. Then he surrendered to General Nelson A. Miles and an army of five thousand soldiers, four hundred Apache scouts, a large civilian militia, and the Mexican army.

General Miles put Geronimo and 340 Apache on a train bound for Fort Marion, Florida. The heat was deadly, and nearly a third of the Apache died. Some were later transferred to Mount Vernon Barracks in Alabama, and a few were even sent home to San Carlos Reservation. Most, including Geronimo, were sent to Fort Sill in Oklahoma in 1894. The old warrior never saw his beloved Apache country again. He died of pneumonia on February 17, 1909. *See also* APACHE.

**GHOST DANCE.** Part of a religious movement that combined Christian ideas with Indian rituals, begun by Wovoka, a Paiute prophet, in 1889. Wovoka, it was said, had spoken to the Great Spirit, who urged the Paiute to be good and to live in peace. He gave Wovoka the dance. If the Paiute danced for five consecutive nights, they would be rewarded with happiness, and the spirits of the dead would be revived.

**The Ghost Dance by the Ogallala Sioux**

The Ghost Dance spread far and wide. It reached the Sioux in South Dakota, who interpreted Wovoka's message to mean the destruction of their white enemies. At Wounded Knee Creek, on December 29, 1890, the Sioux began to dance. The American army ordered them to stop, but they did not. Shots were fired. Two hundred Sioux and sixty soldiers were killed in the melee. *See also* SIOUX.

**GORGET.** A flat ornament made of stone, shell, or metal. One or two holes were cut or drilled through the ornament and threaded with a cord. Men wore gorgets around their necks.

**GREEN CORN DANCE.** The *busk,* or Green Corn Dance, marked the beginning of the new year for the tribes of the American Southeast. Old fires were put out and new ones kindled. Houses were cleaned, and bodies were cleansed by taking the Black Drink. The first corn of the season was harvested, cooked, and eaten. All crimes, except murder, committed during the previous year were forgiven.

**HAIDA.** Several thousand years ago the Haida, braving the waters of Hecate Strait, came upon Lak Haida, the windswept Queen Charlotte Islands. They were greeted there by forests of red cedar, Sitka spruce, and hemlock; by black bears, martens, weasels, sea otters, sea lions, dolphins, and whales; by halibut and black cod, and a variety of mussels, clams, crabs, sea urchins, and scallops; by migrating waterfowl, and by the uncountable salmon that spawned in the rivers. Lak Haida, the newcomers discovered, was an island paradise.

With the onset of spring the Haida pursued the sea lion or ranged the forest for bear and marten. They crossed Hecate Strait to trade with the Tsimshian for eulachon oil, a preservative used in storing salmon, and made preparations for the fishing season. The women picked berries and roots. By late spring the Haida were in their fishing camps. The men netted halibut and black cod; the women cut, cleaned, and hung the fish on racks to dry. By late summer the nets were ready for the pink salmon. Not until late autumn did the Haida return to their big, gable-roofed winter homes.

Winter was an important Haida season. It was the time to carve wooden boxes, masks, and utensils; the time to weave blankets and baskets; the time for art and self expression; the time to participate in the Haida ceremonials,

**A medicine
mask dance
by Haida
Indian leaders**

particularly the potlatch. It was the season to rest, to make merry, and to visit with old friends, kin, and acquaintances.

The Spaniards arrived in Lak Haida in 1774, but the British and the American "Boston Men" made the biggest impact. They came as traders. They introduced the Haida to iron, copper, brass, muskets, powder and shot, beads, trinkets, and rum. In return the Haida offered the prized sea otter pelt, other pelts, and dried salmon stored in wooden boxes. The iron was especially important to the Haida, for from it they could fashion better tools. They could make better canoes, taller and finer totem poles, and better wooden boxes and utensils. Most of the new trade items could also be used in the winter potlatches.

But the newcomers also brought new diseases. In the late eighteenth and early nineteenth centuries, smallpox, measles, and tuberculosis ran rampant through the Haida villages. When the Europeans came, Haida population was estimated at ten thousand. By the turn of the twentieth century Haida numbers had been reduced to 630, and by 1915 to 592—the all-time low. The villages had been reduced from thirty-four to a mere two—Masset and Skidegate. The Haida were in danger of extinction.

Meanwhile the missionaries had come to Lak Haida. Reverend W.H. Collison, an Anglican, was at Masset in 1876. Collison encouraged the Haida to change their life-style. They could no longer create graven images such as totem poles; they could no longer dance their primitive dances; they could no longer keep slaves (Haida society was made up of nobles, commoners, and slaves); they could no longer accept the shaman's "medicine"; and they could no longer participate in the potlatch. The effect of trying to impose Christianity on the Haida was devastating to their culture.

Today the Haida still live in the Queen Charlotte Islands. Many are employed in fishing as of old. Many are employed in the local cannery. They also work in service industries. There is a new vitality in the arts. Robert Davidson carved a totem pole—the first one built in eight decades at Masset—in 1969; he also carried out a training program for aspiring artists. The churches—the Anglican Church at Masset and the United Church of Canada at Skidegate—remain active. The Haida, numbering about one thousand five hundred, are very much alive today. *See also* CHARLES EDENSAW.

**HANDSOME LAKE** (?–1815). An Iroquois (Seneca) prophet. On June 15, 1799, near death, Handsome Lake went into a trance. The spirits who visited him, Handsome Lake said, told him that the Seneca must stop drinking and must no longer practice witchcraft. Three weeks later, in still another trance, Handsome Lake was given the *Gaiwiio,* or the Good Word.

The Good Word, as it developed, was a mixture of Iroquois and Christian teachings: alcohol must be given up, Iroquois men must become farmers, the aged must be cared for, witches must be killed, the good would go to heaven, and the bad to hell.

Although Handsome Lake died in 1815, the Good Word was spread widely. In the middle of the nineteenth century, the Code of Handsome Lake was written down. Today it is the basis of the Iroquois Longhouse Religion. *See also* IROQUOIS *and* LONGHOUSE.

**HOGAN.** The traditional Navaho dwelling. Made with forked poles and covered with branches, brush, and earth, it was semisubterranean, circular, and always faced east. The Navaho say the Holy People built the very first hogan this way. The forked-pole hogan is rarely seen on the Navaho reservation today. Instead, the six- or eight-sided hogan, made with horizontally laid logs and plastered with mud or earth, prevails in the rural areas. In the modern Navaho communities the hogan is no longer used.

**HOPI.** "The peaceful ones" have lived in northeastern Arizona for centuries. Old Oraibi, the oldest of the Hopi villages, was founded in the twelfth century. During the Great Drought in the Southwest (A.D. 1276–1299), many peoples left their pueblos to join the Hopi. Four centuries later, during the Pueblo Revolt against the Spaniards in 1680, Tewa from New Mexico established a village at Hano. All of the newcomers, in time, became Hopi and took part in "the Hopi way."

In the dry, mesa-filled country, the Hopi were floodwater farmers. They raised maize, beans, squash, melons, and cotton in the clan-owned fields. They cared for apple, pear, and peach trees. The men were the farmers. The women had other tasks. They cared for the children and the home, prepared the food (*piki,* a thin bread made from maize meal, was a favorite), and carried water from the springs to the mesa top. They also tended their vegetable gardens and made fine clay pots, bowls, or, occasionally, a coiled basket.

**Hopi maidens**

At the winter solstice, the Hopi ceremonials began. The *Soyal Kachina* was said to emerge from the underworld. When the Soyal *kiva* (a building that is partially or wholly underground) was "opened," the Hopi knew that the course of the sun would be changed, that warmth would come to the fields soon to be planted, and that happiness would come to the Hopi themselves. The Soyal was followed, in February, by the *Powamu,* an initiation ceremony. Then the Kachina clan took over the ceremonial activities until after the *Niman* dance at the summer solstice. The kivas were "closed," and the spirits returned to the underworld.

In the late nineteenth century there were many disturbances in Hopi country. The Navajo attacked "the peaceful ones." And it looked as if the Mormons would descend on the Hopi. In 1882 a reservation was established. Eleven years later, a Mennonite mission was built at Oraibi. Some Hopi bitterly opposed the coming of the Americans; others were quite friendly to the new-comers. At Oraibi the two factions grew further and further apart. Nothing could bring them together. Finally, a push-of-war, in which the two sides stood on either side of a line drawn on the ground and actually pushed each other, was fought between the two. The Conservatives (those who opposed the coming of the Americans) lost and were forced to abandon Old Oraibi. They founded the new town of Hoteville in 1906.

Today the Hopi remain in the old mesa-filled country. There are still those who practice floodwater farming. But much of the Hopi life-style has changed. There are good roads, schools, and dwellings. On Second Mesa a new cultural center was built in 1971. It has a fine hotel, a restaurant, a conference center, craft shops, and a museum. Hopi men work today as carpenters, painters, masons, and mechanics. Hopi women paint and make pots and jewelry. The Hopi Tribal Council may, in the future, derive much money from the coal on Black Mesa and from pressing their land claims before the Indian Claims Commission.

Hopi life has changed; it will continue to change. But the Hopi identity, "the Hopi way," remains. At the winter solstice, say the Hopi, the Soyal continues to emerge each year from the underground.

**INDIAN CLAIMS COMMISSION.** Created by the Act of August 13, 1946. Indian tribes, bands, or any identifiable Indian groups could bring before the commission their claims concerning treaty promises, imposed treaties, or what they considered to be unfair and dishonorable dealings or inadequate payment for land. All claims had to be made within five years, by 1951. It is noteworthy that the commission was not empowered to give land away; awards could be made only in money.

Indian groups had to prove that they had held *aboriginal title* (occupied and used the land exclusively) to the territory in question. If such proof could be found, they would be reimbursed at the market value of the land at the time it was taken from them. Experts (anthropologists, historians, and geographers) were called in to testify. By 1951, 370 claims had been filed.

But the commission's work was not finished by 1951, so its life was extended to 1962 and again to 1978. More than 850 claims were made. Many were rejected. Many awards were made. The Ponca received $2,500. The Crow were awarded more than $10 million in 1961. They distributed their money through a Family Plan Program, each family getting more than $3,000. The remaining money was used for economic development, education, and law and order. The Indians of California received $29 million in 1964, based on the fair market value of their land—47¢ per acre—in 1851. This amounted to only $600 per person.

The Indian Claims Commission no longer exists. Today Indian grievances can be filed in courts ranging from county courts to the United States Supreme Court.

**INDIAN REORGANIZATION ACT (WHEELER-HOWARD ACT).** Part of the New Deal legislation of President Franklin D. Roosevelt and due, in large part, to the persistent work of John Collier, Commissioner of Indian Affairs, the Indian Reorganization Act became law in 1934. The Act provided for Indian freedom in religion and life-style. It permitted the establishment of tribal governments. It ended the selling (allotment) of Indian reservation land. It encouraged the creation of business corporations so that tribal property could be better managed, and it provided funds for small businesses. Bilingual education was provided for, so that Indians could learn their tribal language as well as Spanish and English. The Act also made provisions for better health services.

The Indian Magna Carta, as the Indian Reorganization Act has been called, was accepted by 189 tribes and rejected by 77. The native peoples of Alaska and Oklahoma, not included in the original Act, came under its provisions in 1936.

World War II interrupted the progress being made in Indian communities under the Act. Soon thereafter the government's position once more became one of assimilating the Indian into the American mainstream.

**IROQUOIS.** The Mohawk, Oneida, Onondaga, Cayuga, and Seneca—all Iroquois and all from New York State—often fought among themselves. Blood flowed in Iroquois country. Legend says that Deganawidah, the voice of the Iroquois, and Hiawatha, the Mohawk, pleaded for peace, the Great Peace. When the Onondaga agreed to join their brothers, the Iroquois confederation or *Longhouse* was born around the sixteenth century.

Near the palisaded villages which were often surrounded by moats, the Iroquois planted maize, squash, and beans—the Three Sisters. They hunted deer and bear, caught fish, tapped the sugar maples, and gathered a variety of plant foods.

They fought the French in 1609, and they made friends of the Dutch and English. The Dutch supplied the Iroquois with guns, but it was William Johnson, the Englishman, who provided a long-time alliance in 1722. Meanwhile, the Tuscarora, who had come from the south, had joined the confederation to form the Six Nations.

**A model of
an Iroquois
longhouse**

During the French and Indian War (1754–1763), the Iroquois sided with the English. In the Revolutionary War (1775–1783), the Iroquois found it difficult to choose between the English and the Americans. When American armies invaded Seneca lands and burned their houses and fields, many Iroquois fled to Canada.

Many, of course, remained. On the Allegheny River in Pennsylvania lived Cornplanter and his half brother, the prophet Handsome Lake. It was the latter who, in 1799, urged the Iroquois to return to their old ways, to quit drinking and sinning. He preached the New Religion. Handsome Lake's message spread through Iroquois country. It was widely adopted, and today remains a guiding force in Iroquois life.

In the nineteenth century Iroquois from the Caughnawaga Reserve went to work building bridges. Not afraid of height, they became part of riveting crews. In the 1920s and 1930s a number of the Caughnawaga moved to Brooklyn, New York, and got jobs in the steel industry. To this day they are fine steel-workers. They still maintain ties with the Caughnawaga Reserve.

Another Iroquois reserve is the Six Nations Reserve in Ontario. There are Iroquois reservations in New York State. *See also* HANDSOME LAKE *and* LONGHOUSE.

# K-L

**KARNEE.** The dwelling of the Paiute and other tribes of the Great Basin. A karnee was made by planting twenty-odd willow sticks in a large circle, bending them, and lashing them together with willow withes (flexible branches). Mats were then laid on the willow frame from bottom to top. There were two openings, a smoke hole and a door. The karnee was known as the *wickiup* to white travelers in the Great Basin. *See also* WICKIUP.

**LABRET.** An ornament made of stone, bone, or wood and worn in the lower lip. On the Pacific Northwest Coast, young Tlingit, Haida, and Tsimshian women pushed a small piece of wood through the fatty part of their lower lips. Older women wore a circular piece of wood about a half inch (1.3 cm) thick in their lower lips. It was a mark of distinction.

Labrets have been used for centuries. Stone labrets dating from well before the time of Christ have been found on the Pacific Northwest Coast.

**LONGHOUSE.** The term often applied to the confederation of the Iroquois. Today it refers to the community hall, as in the Tonawanda Longhouse in New York. It also refers to the Longhouse Religion. And, it is the Iroquois house—50 to 100 feet (15 to 30 m) long and 20 feet (6 m) wide, bark covered, and with a vaulted roof—in which a number of related families lived. *See also* IROQUOIS.

**LONG WALK.** The Navaho made the Long Walk in 1864. While American troops fought elsewhere in the opening years of the Civil War, Navaho and Apache warriors raided the nearby pueblos and Mexican and American settlements. To stop the raiding, Gen. James Carleton urged Col. Christopher (Kit) Carson to round up first the Mescalero Apache, and then the Navaho.

Carson's strategy was simple. With seven hundred New Mexico volunteers, he decided to destroy the planted fields and slaughter the sheep by the thousands. Those men who did not surrender would be killed, and the women and children would be taken as prisoners.

Early in 1864 Carson invaded the Canyon de Chelly. He ripped up the maize fields and tore down the peach trees. The Navaho scattered. But those captured were treated well and given food. They began to drift into Fort Defiance, hoping to find peace and security. Others soon followed, twenty-four hundred in the first few weeks and later thousands more.

But Fort Defiance was not the end of their journey; it was only the beginning. On March 6, 1864, the Navaho began the Long Walk—300 miles (483 km) to the Bosque Redondo, a desolate reservation in eastern New Mexico. Four hundred Mescalero were already there; eighty-five hundred Navaho would eventually join them. The humiliation of the walk and the bitter four-year stay near the banks of the Little Pecos were never forgotten by the Navaho.

Not until June 1868 were the Navaho permitted to leave the Bosque Redondo. But by July 20 they were back on a new reservation in the old Navaho country. *See also* NAVAHO.

**MCGILLIVRAY, ALEXANDER** (1759–1793). The son of a Scotchman (Lachlan McGillivray) and a half Creek, half French woman (Sehoy), McGillivray became the Great Beloved Man of the Creeks and a leading diplomat of the Creek Confederacy. He grew up on his father's plantation on the Coosa River in Alabama. As a young man he was educated in a white man's school in Charleston. He worked for a time in Savannah.

When he returned to the Coosa River during the Revolutionary War in 1777 the literate McGillivray became chief of the Creek federation and accepted a British commission as a commissary. He was able to maintain a good relationship with the British throughout the war. By war's end he could muster up to six thousand Creek warriors for battle on short notice.

But the land-hungry Georgians were moving deeper into Creek territory. To stop them, the Creek sought an alliance with the Spaniards to the south (Treaty of Pensacola, June 1, 1784). McGillivray was one of the signers. Before long the Creeks were trading at Panton, Leslie and Company in Pensacola and McGillivray was appointed Spanish commissary to the Creek towns.

McGillivray became an adviser to the Creek *miccos*, or chiefs, and soon earned the Great Beloved Man title. He was able to maintain power by controlling the flow of trade goods from Panton, Leslie and Company and by using, on occasion, his own private police force.

Meanwhile, the Georgians continued to push the Creeks west. McGillivray realized that only the United States government could stop them. At the head of a large Creek delegation McGillivray appeared before Secretary of War Knox and President George Washington. The Treaty of New York was signed on August 7, 1790. The United States was thus committed to the preservation of Creek territory. It was a great victory for McGillivray.

The Great Beloved Man's work was done. He died February 17, 1793, and was buried in the garden of his friend, William Panton, in Pensacola. *See also* CREEKS.

**MAIZE.** Wild maize first appeared in the central highlands of Mexico and the Oaxacan and Mayan highlands. About seven thousand years ago maize was planted for the first time, perhaps in the Tehuacan Valley. The small cobs, only as big as pennies, were chewed for the juice; the remainder was spat away. Eventually maize was crossed with other grasses, and the ears and kernels grew larger. Maize became an important plant food. It began to spread to other areas.

By 3600 B.C. maize was planted near Bat Cave in New Mexico. The plantings later spread to the American Southeast and Northeast, and ultimately to the St. Lawrence Valley. Maize farming also moved to Middle and South America and to the Lesser and Greater Antilles.

In the Arizona desert the Hohokam grew maize under irrigation before the time of Christ, as did the later Pueblo peoples of New Mexico. The Hopi were floodwater farmers. Elsewhere farmers relied on natural rainfall.

The Iroquois had great respect for the spirit of Maize and for the spirits of Beans and Squash. Together they were called the Three Sisters, or Our Life.

**MAYA.** The Indians have lived in Mexico, Guatemala, and Belize for more than four thousand years. In 2400 B.C. Maya were already planting maize at Cuello, in Belize. By 2000 B.C. a courtyard was being laid out for the Cuello ceremonial center. But not until the so-called Maya Classic period, the third to ninth centuries A.D., did Maya civilization reach its zenith.

At Uaxactun and Tikal in the wet Peten, at Yaxchilán and Palenque in the Usumacinta drainage, at Uxmal, Labna, and Cobá in Yucatan and at Cuello, the Maya civilization flourished.

Tikal was, perhaps, the most imposing center. It was protected by an earthen wall and approached by wide causeways. It was dominated by a number of

**A Maya temple**

manmade hills on which tall pyramids stood, crowned by individual temples. Nearby were the palaces. A great central market served the community. There were wares from the mountains and the sea—tobacco, salt, obsidian blades, fish, herbs, quetzal feathers, textiles, gourds, and beeswax candles—all traded for cacao beans, the means of exchange. Notable, too, were the ball courts, where nobility and commoners alike watched the games. In the bustling community and vicinity lived about forty thousand Maya.

The Maya were priest astronomers. They observed eclipses, equinoxes, and solstices. They watched the courses of the moon, the sun, and the planet Venus. They perfected a calendar. Fine artists, potters, and workers in wood, shell, bone, and jade, the Maya were also dedicated to their gods.

But the Maya Classic came to an end in the tenth century. We are not sure why. Perhaps there was not enough food, or diseases may have taken a horrible toll. Perhaps an enemy destroyed them. We do know that the ceremonial centers were deserted and Tikal was abandoned.

Today the Maya still live in Mexico, Guatemala, and Belize. Many are peasant farmers and factory employees.

**MENOMINEE.** The Algonquian-speaking Menominee lived in the forested lake country between the Escanaba and Milwaukee rivers in what is now Michigan and Wisconsin. Their winter villages were made up of dome-shaped, bark- or mat-covered wigwams, a number of sweat lodges and menstrual huts, and a medicine lodge. In summer they lived in open and airy rectangular log houses with high sloping roofs. Minikani, the chief village, stood near the mouth of the Menominee River.

The Menominee gathered wild rice in autumn and a wide variety of nuts, roots, and berries in season. They netted and speared sturgeon and caught trout, whitefish, perch, and pike. They snared ducks and geese and hunted deer, bison, moose, elk, and small game.

They knew much about the world. Their traders brought copper from Lake Superior and catlinite, for the manufacture of pipes, from Minnesota. Their warriors were familiar with the Great Lakes area and the country west to the Mississippi River.

The French arrived in 1634. For more than a century French traders, missionaries, and soldiers had a strong influence on the Indians. The Menominee were urged to pursue beaver for pelts; they learned to use iron kettles, hatchets, swords, and knives; they were introduced to the Catholic faith; and they became involved in numerous wars. The Menominee also traded with the British, who gave them guns and rum and who involved them in the War of 1812. The impact of Americans on the Menominee was devastating.

Land-hungry Americans poured into Wisconsin. In the treaties of 1831 and 1836 with the United States, the Menominee gave up much of their territory. In 1848 they ceded *all* of their land in Wisconsin. But in 1854 they were awarded a tract on Wolf River—the Menominee Reservation.

In the quarter century that followed, life changed drastically for the Menominee. Frame houses were built; Menominee children began to go to school; and American-style clothing was introduced, especially at Keshena, the chief settlement. The Menominee tried their hands at farming and lumbering. They hired out as laborers in white-owned lumber mills. By the 1880s there were those who worshipped Indian gods and those who followed the Catholic faith, thereby creating deep gulfs in Menominee society.

After the turn of the twentieth century the United States, employing Indian workers, built a sawmill at Neopit, which was to become the largest Menominee settlement. But tuberculosis and other diseases caused by the consumption of alcohol began to plague the tribe. A Catholic hospital was finally built at Keshena in 1926.

The worst was yet to come. In 1954 the United States sought the termination of reservation status for many tribes, a move that would end federal supervision and protection. The Menominee Reservation, in fact, was terminated in 1961, and the reservation was organized as Menominee County, Wisconsin.

Menominee County's land, lumber mill, and forest areas fell under the management of Menominee Enterprises, Inc. (MEI), an all-Indian body. But Menominee County was poor. Family income was the lowest in the state; unemployment was the highest among Wisconsin's counties. MEI could not raise enough tax money to meet its obligations. Land was sold to non-Menominee in order to raise money, but Menominee tribal members became angry. Only a reversal of the termination policy could save the Menominee.

On December 22, 1973, the Menominee Restoration Act was passed, and the Menominee were restored to full tribal status. By 1975 they were authorized to establish a tribal police force. In 1976 they adopted a new constitution.

Today there are more than five thousand Menominee. More than half live on the reservation. The others have long since moved to Milwaukee, Chicago, and other urban areas. *See also* OSHKOSH.

**MICMAC.** The Algonquian-speaking Micmac lived in Nova Scotia, neighboring New Brunswick, Prince Edward Island, and the Gaspé Peninsula of Quebec. They may have been observed by the Norsemen about A.D. 1000 and most assuredly by John Cabot in 1497 on voyages along the east coast of North America.

In winter the Micmac hunted moose, caribou, bear, and beaver with bows and arrows; in spring they fished the rivers for herring, sturgeon, and salmon and moved to the seashore to gather shellfish and search for seals. They lived in lightweight conical wigwams covered with birch bark, skins, or woven mats. The Micmac made sturdy canoes and baskets, boiled their food in wooden troughs, and fashioned cooking pots from clay.

The Micmac had no tribal structure. They lived in small bands and met only for summer gatherings and such ceremonials as healings, marriages, funerals, thanksgivings, and waging war. However, they did recognize the leader of the Cape Breton Island band as a leading chieftain.

In the sixteenth century the French arrived. The Micmac, who numbered about three thousand, became fur traders and were sought out by the Jesuit missionaries. They were exposed to European diseases. Micmac women and French men intermarried. Pushed into the wars of the eighteenth century, their numbers began to decline.

Under the British after the Treaty of Paris in 1763, conditions were a little better. But the British put greater demands on the Micmac for territory, particularly in the nineteenth century, and the Micmac were driven deeper into the bush.

With the twentieth century, Micmac life changed in many ways. In the Restigouche community at Chaleur Bay, for example, a sawmill was built in 1902; it flourished until it was destroyed by fire in 1931. An Indian Day School was opened in 1903. Micmac served in the armed forces during World War I. There were jobs for the Micmac in lumber camps, on log drives, and during wheat harvests. During the Great Depression they found employment in the potato harvests of Aroostook County, Maine. The old ways of Micmac life were all but gone.

Following World War II the Micmac moved in increasing numbers to the United States. Today, one-third of their adult population live and work in American urban communities in Maine, Connecticut, Massachusetts, and New Jersey. Being outsiders, they have suffered from unemployment and racism. They continue, of course, to maintain their identity through ties with the Canadian reserves. The Micmac population today is about ten thousand.

**NAVAHO.** The Navaho have lived in the Four Corners area of Colorado, Utah, Arizona, and New Mexico for centuries. They were already skilled hunters, gatherers, and raiders upon arrival. They raided the nearby pueblos and also traded with them. During the Pueblo Revolt of 1680, many Pueblo peoples fled to Navaho country; the Navaho learned about floodwater farming, weaving, making pots, and sand painting from the new arrivals. They began to use various Pueblo masks and altars, and they adopted the clan system. In the eighteenth century, after raiding the Spanish settlements, the Navaho learned to care for horses, sheep, and goats. All that they learned from Pueblos and Spaniards alike would become part of the Navaho way.

Navaho settlements were made up of a number of forked-stick *hogans* covered with branches, grasses, and earth; sweat lodges; and a ceremonial house. Nearby were sheep corrals, pastures for horses, and fields of maize, squash, beans, and watermelons. Each settlement was led by the *natani,* a much respected man well versed in the Navaho ceremonials. There were also war leaders, who, in the nineteenth century, led war parties against the Spaniards, Mexicans, and Americans.

The United States built Fort Defiance in the heart of Navaho country in 1852. But the Indian fighting continued. In 1863 Kit Carson was ordered to round up the Navaho and bring them to the Bosque Redondo on the Pecos River. On

**Navaho women**

March 6, 1864, the Long Walk — 300 miles (483 km) — began. It was agonizing, as was their stay on the "reservation." Only after four years of misery were eight thousand Navaho permitted to return to their old land and a new reservation.

By 1890 there were twenty thousand Navaho, and by 1930 there were forty thousand. The land could no longer support them. Government officials suggested that the Navaho spread themselves over the reservation and reduce the number of livestock. In fact, thousands of animals were killed and no compensation was offered. Navaho bitterness was widespread.

Only after World War II did the situation in Navaho country improve. The Navaho built schools including Rough Rock Demonstration School, and, in 1968, the Navaho Community College. They have built a hospital and health facilities and improved the roads. They have supported a Navaho Indian Irrigation Project and a Navaho Forest Management Plan. And they have derived millions of dollars in royalties from coal, oil, natural gas, and uranium on and off their reservation.

Today the Navaho is the richest and largest (130,000) of the American Indian tribes. From the modern, hoganlike council chamber at Window Rock, tribal members are helping to plan the Navaho future. *See also* LONG WALK.

**NEZ PERCÉ.** The Nez Percé, (a French term meaning "pierced noses") were fisherfolk and gatherers of the Western Plateau in what is now Washington, Oregon, and Idaho. In spring the women left their riverside villages for the hillsides to dig out the roots of the cowish, which they steamed or boiled into mush. They made cowish root biscuits which could last for months. In late summer the women gathered the bulbs of the blue camas. These, too, were steamed and made into enough small loaves to last the winter. Meanwhile, the men were busy with spears, nets, and traps catching salmon, the staple in the Nez Percé diet.

**A Nez Percé boy**

When Lewis and Clark visited the Nez Percé in 1805 and 1806, the Indians lived in sixty or more villages and numbered about six thousand. They owned large horse herds and bred the Appaloosa. This spotted horse was traded to the Crow across the Rockies and to other tribes at the Dalles (Columbia River) trading center.

Then the American settlers began to arrive. The missionary, Henry H. Spalding, and his wife Eliza led the way in 1836. A reservation was established in 1855. After the discovery of gold in 1860, miners and their camp followers moved into the reservation area. The Nez Percé were greatly disturbed. By 1863 the reservation area was much reduced by treaty, and many of the Nez Percé were ready for war.

The situation grew worse. In 1877 the Nez Percé decided to abandon their reservation. Men, women, and children started out over the Lolo Trail. They cut through Yellowstone National Park and moved up the Clark Fork. Many died. Near Bear Paw Mountain in Montana they were caught by General Nelson A. Miles. Their leader, Chief Joseph, was forced to surrender.

Many of the Nez Percé later returned to their old homes near Lapwai. In 1933 they formed their own tribal government. In 1951 they were awarded $7,650,000 by the Indian Claims Commission for the land that had been taken from them. Today fifteen hundred Nez Percé still live near their old haunts in the Western Plateau. *See also* CHIEF JOSEPH.

**OSCEOLA** (1803–1838). A Florida Seminole, a fighter for freedom. In 1832 at the signing of the Treaty of Payne's Landing, the Seminoles were forced to leave Florida for Indian Territory in Oklahoma. Some refused to go. In 1835 the American Army was sent against the Seminoles in what was known as the Second Seminole War. Osceola, Tiger Tail, Alligator, Wildcat, and Halek attacked the army, retreated, and attacked again. But in 1837 Osceola was captured and put in jail. He died in 1838 at Fort Moultrie in Charleston Harbor. *See also* SEMINOLES.

**OSHKOSH** (1795–1858). Served as head chief of the Menominee for more than thirty years. At age seventeen he was already a warrior. He fought against the Americans in the War of 1812 at the British capture of Fort Mackinaw; he took part in the attacks on Fort Meigs on the Maumee and Fort Stephenson on the Sandusky in 1814. When Americans erected a new fort on Green Bay in 1817, Oshkosh was greatly disturbed. In 1821 Oshkosh became leader of the Menominee Bear Clan, and in 1827 he became head chief of the tribe.

Oshkosh always firmly opposed giving up Menominee land to the United States, but in treaties signed in 1831 and 1836 the Menominee gave up much of their historic territory. In 1848 they were pressured into giving up all of their land in Wisconsin in exchange for acreage in Minnesota. The dismayed Oshkosh signed the treaty. But in 1850 he went to Washington to plead the Menominee case before President Millard Fillmore.

The President agreed to permit the Menominee to stay in Wisconsin until June 1, 1851. Three years later, in 1854, the Menominee were awarded a tract of land on Wolf River, Wisconsin, where the Menominee Reservation remains to this very day. Oshkosh had won the most important battle of his life. *See also* MENOMINEE.

**PAIUTE.** Gatherers in the semiarid Great Basin. They collected rye seeds on the mountain slopes in spring; edible roots, wild berries, and even grasshoppers in summer; and piñon nuts on the high slopes in the fall. Surpluses were stored in pits at the winter settlements.

Life was best in the well watered country where fish, ducks, geese, and pelicans were available; it was most difficult in the very dry areas where plant and animal resources were limited.

Europeans and Americans came late to the Paiute country. Only the coming of the fur trappers and gold seekers, and the discovery of the Comstock Lode in 1859 changed the lives of the Paiute rapidly. Miners and settlers poured into Nevada. The Central Pacific Railroad was built right through Paiute territory. A reservation was created. There was drought, typhoid, and measles.

The Paiute prophets, Wodziwob and Wovoka, predicted that happiness would come to the Paiute and the dead would be returned to earth if the Paiute danced the Ghost Dance. They did, each year from 1869 to 1872 and again in 1890. But the dancing brought little happiness, and the dead did not return.

On October 29, 1906, the Walker River reservation was opened to white settlement. Whites began to lease the Paiute acres and to open businesses on Paiute land.

Today there are fourteen reservations and twelve colonies in the Nevada Indian Agency. There are Paiute at Pyramid Lake, at Walker River, in Carson City, in the Reno ghetto, and elsewhere in urban America. *See also* SARAH WINNEMUCCA.

**PAPAGO.** The Piman-speaking Papago, descendants of the Hohokam, lived—and still live—in the desert of south-central Arizona and northern Sonora in Mexico. Fine farmers, the Papago raised maize, beans, squash, and cotton under irrigation; they gathered the mesquite pod, the prickly pear, the fruit of the saguaro, and the buds of the cholla cactus; they hunted the deer, rabbit, and squirrel and dug desert rats out of their burrows.

Water is the key to life in the hot, dry Papago country, often called Papagueria. Thus, the Indians built their summer villages and planted their crops where water flowed from the mountains onto flat ground. The men were the planters; the women were responsible for the harvests. A winter village, also located near an adequate water supply, was maintained in the foothills. The Papago moved each year between summer and winter settlements. When water supplies failed, they moved to other locations within the Papagueria.

Father Eusebio Francisco Kino, a Jesuit, and the Spaniards arrived in the Papagueria in 1687. In the years that followed, the mission system was introduced. The Papago learned about the Catholic faith. They also learned to plant wheat, barley, chick peas, onions, and melons, and to care for horses and cattle. In 1821 the Papago country became a part of Mexico, and in 1854 much of the Papagueria was sold to the United States.

Small reservations were created in 1874 at San Xavier and in 1884 at Gila Bend. But only five hundred Papago populated them. More than five thousand preferred to live in their own *rancherias* or settlements—in dome-shaped brush huts, often thatched or covered with earth—widely scattered over the Papagueria. Not until 1917 was the present-day Sells reservation created.

On the reservations the villages are still widely-spaced, but the dome-shaped houses are no more. Instead, one often finds one- or two-room houses, flat or gable-roofed, made of ocotillo or adobe brick. A ramada is occasionally attached. Water comes from deep wells. Vegetables, beans, tortillas, and coffee are important elements in the Papago diet. Malnutrition, however, is common.

The reservations are divided today into eleven districts. Each district elects a council to govern itself. Each district also sends two delegates to a tribal council, but the council often finds it difficult to reach a consensus.

Less than half of the Papago, who number more than twelve thousand today, live on the reservations. The others have moved to the commercial farming areas of Coolidge and Marana, to the Ajo copper mining area, and to Tucson and Phoenix. Most Papago income is derived from off-reservation sources, but the off-reservation Papago maintain close ties with the reservations.

**QUANAH PARKER** (1845–1911). The son of a Comanche chief, Nokoni, and a white woman, Cynthia Ann Parker, who was taken captive at age twelve during a Comanche raid on Parker's Fort in 1835. Cynthia Parker was later recaptured by Texas soldiers in 1860 but died soon thereafter. Quanah grew to manhood among his father's people, the Quahadi Comanche. He spent his early years as a hunter, warrior, and raider. He learned well the Comanche life-style. After his father's death he became a Quahadi chieftain.

In 1868 the Comanche, Cheyenne, Arapaho, Kiowa, and Kiowa Apache signed the Medicine Lodge Treaty, which assigned them to a reservation north of Red River in Oklahoma. The Quahadi did not sign the treaty. They continued to hunt bison in the Texas panhandle. In 1874, with white bison hunters entrenched at Adobe Walls, Quanah Parker, the Quahadi, and their allies attacked in force. But the fort did not fall. Before long the frontier was in flames. The Quahadi did not move to the reservation until 1875.

Quanah Parker, with the consent of the Indian agent, permitted Texas cattlemen to graze their herds on the reservation. He was paid well for the privilege. He later favored leasing the land to the cattlemen so that all of the people on the reservation could profit.

By the 1880s Quanah Parker was the leading spokesman for the Comanche. He worked with the Indian agents to bring better education, housing, and agriculture to the reservation. He served as judge on a Court of Indian Offenses from 1886–1898 and made repeated trips to Washington on behalf of his people.

Quanah Parker lived to see, to his dismay, the allotment, or sale, of the reservation land. By 1906 the Comanche held no land in common. Quanah Parker himself had a large house surrounded by cultivated fields near Fort Sill, Oklahoma. At the time of his death on February 23, 1911, he was still known as the principal chief of the Comanche. No successor was appointed. *See also* COMANCHE.

**PEMMICAN.** A long-lasting food made from pounded meat, berries, and fat. Bison meat and fat, cherries and other wild fruits, and bone marrow made up the pemmican of the Great Plains tribes; in Canada dry caribou meat was mixed with fat to make the northern tribes' staple.

**POCAHONTAS** (1595–1617). Powhatan's beautiful daughter who helped save the Jamestown colony. When Captain John Smith was captured in 1608 and brought to Powhatan's village, he was set before an altar stone to be killed. Pocahontas covered Captain Smith's body with her own and saved his life. She convinced Powhatan to send supplies to those starving at Jamestown and thus saved the English settlement.

Pocahontas became a convert to Christianity. She married the English tobacco planter, John Rolfe, in 1614. As Lady Rebecca Rolfe she traveled to England. She died there in 1617.

**POMO.** The Hokan-speaking Pomo were at home on Clear Lake, the Russian River drainage, and along the central coast of California. In the late eighteenth century the Pomo lived in some seventy villages—each with dome- or cone-shaped houses, a semisubterranean dance house, a sweat house, and a number of granaries where food was stored.

At Clear Lake the food resources were especially abundant. There were fish, roots, freshwater clams, waterfowl, elk, deer, cherries, piñon nuts, and acorns, the all-important staple in the Pomo diet. Gathered by the women, assisted by the men and children, in autumn, the acorns were dried, hulled, and pounded into flour. Hot water, poured over the flour, helped to remove the poisonous tannic acid. Water was added and the mixture cooked and served as a gruel or porridge. Acorn meal was also made into unleavened cakes.

The Pomo world was full of evil spirits, ghosts, and the fear of being poisoned. They relied on the medicine man, who knew the proper curing songs and could suck evils from the body. If death occurred, after a four-day mourning period the body was cremated. The possessions of the dead were burned.

The Pomo took part in the *Kuksu* cult and the Ghost Ceremony. They traded among themselves and with their neighbors, the Yuki, Wintun, and Miwok. The men fought wars, played games (the grass game and shinny were favorites), ran footraces, and gambled; the women were the makers of the finest baskets (coiled and twill-plaited) made in Indian America.

In the nineteenth century Russians and Spaniards both arrived in Pomo country, but their impact on Pomo life was slight. Americans arrived after the discovery of gold in California in 1848, and Pomo numbers declined drastically due to disease, starvation, and wanton killing. In 1856 more than two thousand were placed on the Mendocino Reserve, where they stayed until 1867. When they returned to their old landholdings, they found them occupied. The Pomo became squatters, and found work in the grain and hop fields. Dejected, the Pomo were swept up in the Ghost Dance and the cults that emerged from it. They hoped and dreamed that the whites would disappear and Indian ways would return. Instead, the Pomo became wage laborers. Some raised vegetables. Others hunted and gathered as of old. During the Great Depression in the 1930s, there were jobs with the WPA (Works Progress Administration) and CCC (Civilian Conservation Corps).

World War II sent the Pomo into the armed forces. Many moved to the cities. There were those, of course, who remained near the old haunts of Clear Lake and Russian River.

At the turn of the nineteenth century the Pomo numbered more than fourteen thousand. They number fewer than a thousand today.

**Pontiac**

**PONTIAC** (1720–1769). The capable strategist who united the Great Lakes tribes, and others, in the struggle against the British. Born of a Chippewa mother and Ottawa father, Pontiac grew to manhood near French-held Detroit. There the neighboring tribes exchanged pelts for French trade goods—especially weapons. In times of need the French traders often supplied the Indians with food and credit for other necessities.

During the French and Indian War (1754–1763), however, British forces captured many of the French forts in the west, including Detroit. Pontiac fled from the British invaders, but for those who remained there were hard times. British agents charged high prices for shoddy trade goods. And the gifts of food and credit, given cheerfully by the French, were not forthcoming from the new conquerors. What is more, the British had come to settle and stay.

Pontiac struck back. He brought the Ottawa, Potawatomi, Wyandot, Shawnee, Miami, Kickapoo, Seneca, and Delaware tribes together and with brilliant oratory urged them to strike at the British in unison. From Fort Pitt to beyond Lake Michigan, the British were to be driven from the country.

Pontiac's early successes were spectacular. In the spring and summer of 1763, the Indian allies, striking swiftly at the forts closest to them, captured eight of the twelve British bastions in the west. The garrisons at Sandusky, Presque Island, and Michilimackinac were destroyed. Pontiac himself laid siege to Detroit—a siege that lasted for six long months.

The British, well supplied with arms and men, finally broke the siege in 1765. Pontiac, heartbroken, went west to Illinois. He tried hard to rally the tribes, pointing out that eighteen nations were at his beck and call. But his influence was already much diminished. In 1766 at Oswego, New York, Pontiac signed a treaty of peace and amity with the British. His dream of crushing his enemies and driving them from the west had come to an end.

On a visit to Cahokia, Illinois, on April 20, 1769, the great leader of the Indian allies was clubbed and stabbed to death.

**POPULATION.** It is difficult to estimate the population of the American Indians through time. Many estimates have been made, some conservative, others quite liberal. In recent years experts have revised their estimates upward.

The best liberal estimates range between forty million and a hundred million for the population of North and South America and the Greater and Lesser Antilles at the time of the Spanish conquests. Those who use a population of ninety million claim that the greatest numbers lived in Mexico (thirty million) and the Andes of Peru and Ecuador (thirty million). The population of North America (north of the Rio Grande) was just under ten million.

The conservatives, who believe these figures are inflated, use estimates of between one million and ten million for the same time period.

Wars, forced labor, induced migrations, and disease cut heavily into Indian numbers. By the late seventeenth century, populations in Mexico (1.5 million) and Peru-Ecuador (1.5 million) had fallen to their all-time lows. In North America the all-time low, just more than 500,000, was reached about 1930.

Today Indian numbers are increasing. While the United States population is growing at a rate of 1 percent per year, the Indian population is growing at a rate of 2.5 percent, the highest growth rate for any group in the country. There are already more than 800,000 Indians in the United States; there are more than 250,000 in Canada.

**POTLATCH.** A community ceremonial of the Pacific Northwest Coast that enabled chiefs and others to compete for status or prestige. A chief would demonstrate his wealth by giving away—or even destroying—his property—canoes, copper plates, blankets. His finest gifts would go to his highest-ranking guests; his lesser gifts would go to nobles of lower rank. Everyone except the slaves received a gift. The naming of a newborn child, the arrival of puberty, a wedding, or the erection of a totem pole all called for a potlatch. The ceremony was often accompanied by singing, dancing, and feasting.

**PUEBLO REVOLT** (1680). In New Mexico in 1680 the Pueblos, under Popé of San Juan and Naranjo, the mulatto, revolted against Spanish rule. The Spaniards were crushed in the fighting. Twenty-one of thirty-three missions were destroyed; 375 civilians were killed.

The Spanish survivors took refuge in Santa Fe, but the Pueblos laid siege to the Spanish capital. After more bloody fighting the Spaniards were forced to withdraw. They fled to El Paso.

The Indians destroyed the Catholic images, the crosses, and the bells. Popé urged them to wash their bodies with yucca root to rid themselves of the holy waters of baptism. He urged them to take new wives.

But the Pueblos did not destroy everything that was Spanish. They continued to use the horse and the Spanish cart. They retained the cattle. Many continued to speak Spanish. They grew Spanish crops and used the church buildings for other purposes.

Not until 1692 did Diego de Vargas reconquer the Pueblos.

# Q-R

**QUAPAW.** These Indians left their Ohio River Valley homes early in the seventeenth century. They split from their Siouxan-speaking brother tribes, the Omaha, Osage, Kansa, and Ponca, and moved south along the Mississippi River. In the Arkansas-Mississippi River drainage they established their villages and came to be known as ''quapaw,'' the Downstream People.

In their newfound land the Downstream People planted their crops (maize, squash, and beans), fished, searched the neighboring forest for wild fruits and nuts, and hunted bear, deer, wildcat, and rabbit. Before long Quapaw hunting parties were making forays well into Oklahoma to kill the bison.

Father Jacques Marquette and Louis Joliet discovered the Quapaw villages (rectangular shaped, arch-roofed houses covered with cypress bark and cane mats; a ceremonial house; and the flat-topped leader's house) in 1673. The Downstream People smoked the calumet with Robert Cavelier Sieur de la Salle in 1682. And before 1763—when, by the Treaty of Paris, France was driven from North America—French traders and French trade goods were welcome in the Quapaw villages. But the French presence was not altogether a healthy one for the Downstream People. Smallpox ravaged the Quapaw villages and the population fell from nearly ten thousand to seven hundred.

The Spaniards who followed offered presents, medals, and trade goods to the Quapaw. They stationed gunboats in the Mississippi to counter a British threat, and built a fort in Quapaw country. But these events were overcome by the coming of the Americans after the Louisiana Purchase in 1803.

With the Treaty of 1818, the Quapaw ceded most of their old hunting ground, eight hundred square miles (2,072 sq km) to the United States. In return, the Downstream People were awarded a reservation south of the Arkansas River. Six years later, in the Treaty With the Quapaw, (1824), the reservation lands were taken away, and the Quapaw were forced to migrate to the Caddo country on Red River. At least a quarter of the tribe, unhappy in Caddo country, risked returning to Arkansas. Thus the Downstream People were divided into factions.

Once more the United States prevailed. The Quapaw in Arkansas were asked to move to a new reservation in Indian Territory in 1833. Many made the move, but the Quapaw on Red River refused, for the most part, to join them. The Quapaw attempted to survive in their new environment in Indian Territory.

Because there were only about forty Quapaw on the new reservation, the Quapaw began to adopt non-Quapaw into their tribe. Thus, on October 8, 1889, there were 124 ''Quapaw'' on the tribal rolls. And in 1893 the Quapaw began to allot their reservation lands—two hundred acres to each member of the tribe—without government approval. Leftover acres were also alloted. They set aside four hundred acres for schools and ten acres for the Catholic church.

In the years that followed a number of Quapaw became quite wealthy; at least one became a millionaire. The Indians made money by mining lead and zinc and by leasing agricultural land.

In 1947 the Downstream People filed a claim before the Indian Claims Commission, asking for the value in dollars of the land taken from them by the United States in the treaties of 1818 and 1824. The tribe was awarded nearly $1 million in 1954. In 1961 there were 1,199 Quapaw eligible for benefits.

**RED CLOUD** (1822–1909). A Sioux warrior chief of the Oglala Teton. He grew up near the forks of the Platte River in Nebraska. In 1865, when white Americans began constructing a road through the Sioux hunting grounds, between Fort Laramie, Wyoming, and the Montana gold fields, Red Cloud intercepted them. But he permitted the work to continue. In 1866 Americans rebuilt and garrisoned Fort Reno and established forts Kearny and C.F. Smith. Red Cloud could bear it no longer. He and two thousand warriors harassed the roadbuilders and soldiers and prevented supplies and emigrants from reaching the forts.

They routed an army detachment of eighty-one men, all of whom were killed. Red Cloud and his warriors did not let up. Not a single wagon was allowed to pass.

A commission appointed in 1868 finally came to terms with Red Cloud. But the Oglala chief insisted that the three forts be abandoned; he insisted, too, that no further work be done on the new road through Sioux country. The commission had to agree. Only then did Red Cloud sign the Treaty of Fort Laramie on November 6, 1868.

Thereafter Red Cloud lived in peace. On a visit to the east President Ulysses S. Grant awarded him a medal, which he proudly wore. He did not take part in the Sioux wars of 1876 (his son, also known as Red Cloud, did) or 1890. Much respected, the finest of Sioux warriors died blind and decrepit on the Pine Ridge Reservation in South Dakota on December 10, 1909. *See also* SIOUX (DAKOTA).

**RELIGION.** For the most part, Indians believed that there were good and bad spirits. In order to have harmony in the world one had to please the spirits. This could be done through offerings and prayer, sacrifices and charms, and the singing of sacred songs. There was power in animals, in men (shamans), and in deities. Some tribes believed in an all-powerful force in the universe—the *manito* of the Algonquians, the *wakanda* of the Sioux, and the *orenda* of the Iroquois. The Creeks understood the power as the "Master of Life," who breathed life into the Creek people and into the animals of the forest.

Religion was both an individual and a group matter. On the Great Plains, personal power was gained through a vision quest. If the quest was successful, the young man reaching adulthood or the warrior seeking to collect coups would gain a guardian spirit who would protect him. The young man would get his medicine bundle, the source of his power that would help him ward off the bad spirits and bring him good fortune.

The group religious activities among the tribes in the Southeast, Northeast, and Southwest were very elaborate. The priests and medicine societies sought to bring meaning to the universe, rain to the planted fields, victories to the warriors, and successes to the hunters.

Hopi religion, for example, was concerned with healing and, especially, with the bringing of rain. The Hopi priests appealed to the kachinas and held numerous ceremonials. The Snake and Antelope dances were held in an effort to bring water to the fields. Zuni kachinas sang sacred songs or prayed for rain and the growth of crops. The medicine societies at Cochiti were also concerned with healing, controling the weather, and the well-being of the Cochiti themselves.

With regard to the meaning of the universe, most tribes have stories that deal with the creation of the world, their own creation and migration, and what the end of the world will be like. The Tewa of San Juan Pueblo say that they began life under a lake to the north. They emerged through the *sipapu,* or the earth's navel, and moved south along the Rio Grande, where they established their villages. At Zuni they talk about the death of the world. Once soft and wet, the world is now becoming old and dry. The famine is upon us. All manmade things will rise up against us, and hot rain will fall. The world will die.

A bison dance to bring success in hunting

**Cocopa Reservation in Arizona**

**RESERVATION.** A tract of land owned by a tribe or tribes but held in trust by the federal or a state government for the tribe's use and benefit. The first reservation was established at Brotherton, Burlington County, New Jersey, in 1758. It was a dismal failure. By 1802 all the occupants had left.

Between 1786 and 1871 numerous reservations, particularly in the West, were set aside by treaty. Among them were the Ute Reservation created on October 7, 1863, and the Navaho Reservation created on June 1, 1868. Other reservations set aside by executive order included San Carlos for Apache on November 9, 1871, and for Hopi on December 16, 1882. Still others were set aside by purchase or by act of Congress.

Reservations still exist. They are homes and refuges for the Indian people. The Indian is free to live on the reservation or to move away from it. He or she can go to a school on the reservation or to a school elsewhere. He or she can work on the reservation or leave it for a job elsewhere. The tribes have rights on the reservation lands, including ownership rights to minerals and timber, the right to govern, and, on many reservations, the right to have police. Because the land is held in trust by the government, neither tribes nor individuals can sell reservation land.

Some reservations are quite small. On the other hand the Navaho Reservation, the largest in the United States, covers 25,000 square miles; (64,750 sq km); it entirely surrounds the Hopi Reservation. Some reservations are poor, and others are quite wealthy. The Osage Reservation, for example, is blessed with rich oil fields; the Crow Reservation, with ample supplies of coal; and the Navaho Reservation, with rich deposits of coal, oil, natural gas, and uranium.

But for most reservations poverty is still the rule. Unemployment rates are high, and young people tend to seek jobs in the cities. Education and health services lag behind the national average. The reservation seems to be the abode of the very young and the very old. Yet, the reservation remains a key to Indian identity. *See also* RESERVE.

**RESERVE.** The Canadian term for reservation. Louis XIV, the King of France, set aside the first land for Indian use in Quebec in 1680. Under the English, the Six Nations (Iroquois) were awarded a reserve in Ontario for their loyalty during the Revolutionary War. The Canadian government made no treaties with the Indians until 1850. By signing treaties the Indian tribes were able to use the reserve land but gave up title to it; actual ownership was retained by the Canadian government.

Today there are over 250,000 Indians in Canada, about 75 percent of whom live on reserves. They are dispersed in 561 communities or bands. The estate of the Masset Band (Haida), for example, consists of twenty-six pieces of land with an area of more than 2,200 acres. *See also* RESERVATION.

**ROSS, JOHN** (1790–1866). The son of a Scottish immigrant and his part-Cherokee wife. As a youth he went to school in Kingston, Tennessee. In 1809 he was sent on a Cherokee mission to Indian Territory. He fought in the Creek Wars in 1813–1814 and served on the Cherokee Council. From 1828 to 1839 he was the Principal Chief of the Cherokee.

During those years Ross fought hard against President Andrew Jackson's Indian Removal Act of May 28, 1830. He pleaded the Cherokee case in Washington in 1832 and 1833. The Cherokee, he noted, were a civilized people. They had schools, churches, and magnificent farms. They could read and write. They had their own newspaper. But President Jackson stood firm for Cherokee removal which was provided for in the Treaty of New Echota signed in 1835. A petition against the treaty, with more than fifteen thousand signatures, did not help. The Cherokee were forced to move west over the "Trail of Tears" in 1838 and 1839. One of the victims of the journey was Ross's wife, Quatie, who was buried in Little Rock, Arkansas, on February 1, 1839.

Ross lived on in Indian Territory. He tried to remain neutral during the Civil War, but the Cherokee did serve with the Confederate Army. He died in Washington, D.C., on August 1, 1866. *See also* CHEROKEE *and* TRAIL OF TEARS.

# S

**SACAGAWEA** (1784–1812 or 1884). A Shoshone who accompanied Meriwether Lewis and William Clark on their journey to the Pacific Ocean from 1804 to 1806. Captured by the Crow and sold to the Hidatsa, the young Shoshone maiden was finally purchased by the French-Canadian trapper, Toussaint Charbonneau, who became her husband. When Charbonneau was hired as guide and interpreter for Lewis and Clark, Sacagawea was given the opportunity of her lifetime.

She served Lewis and Clark well. When a boat carrying the records of the expedition turned over, Sacagawea saved them. At her home, a Shoshone village where Cameahwait, her brother, was the chief, she allowed no harm to come to the white men. She urged her brother to supply Lewis and Clark with horses and food for the journey through the Rocky Mountain passes. Her bravery, endurance, the care she gave to her infant son Baptiste, born on the trip, and her quiet ways were an inspiration for all in the Lewis and Clark party.

In 1809 William Clark brought the Charbonneaus to St. Louis. In 1811 they once more traveled west with the Manuel Lisa expedition. Baptiste was left at home. William Clark later adopted Baptiste.

We are not certain about Sacagawea's death. A Manuel Lisa clerk reported that she died on December 20, 1812, a young woman of twenty-five. There are those who say that Sacagawea returned to her home village, moved with the villagers to the Wind River Reservation in Wyoming, and died there at a hundred years old on April 9, 1884, at Fort Washakie.

**SCALPING.** The practice of removing a portion of skin, with the hair attached, from an enemy's head. The scalp served as a trophy. The practice was widespread in eastern North America among the Iroquois and Creek; it later spread to the bison hunters of the Great Plains and was known among the Pueblos and on the Northwest Coast.

A fallen enemy was often scalped. Quick knife strokes were made near the crown of the head, and a tug was made at the scalplock. The clean scalp was sacrificed to the sun, the water, or to other deities.

The Crow held a three-day ceremonial in honor of a newly taken scalp. They danced and sang. The scalp was carried on a pole through the encampment. The peaceful Hopi often scalped their enemies. They, too, carried the scalps into their villages on poles. The Tlingit took scalps, but they impaled heads, rather than scalps, on poles.

Scalping increased with the coming of the Europeans and Americans. The newcomers offered generous bounties for the scalps of their enemies.

**An Indian scalping his enemy**

**A Seminole
dwelling**

**SEMINOLES.** The Seminoles of South Florida, it is believed, were derived from the Creeks. The name itself may mean ''runaways'' or ''wild people''—those who left the Creek towns in Alabama and Georgia.

In the First Seminole War in 1818, Andrew Jackson drove the Seminoles deep into Florida. When the United States purchased Florida from Spain in 1819, American settlers drove the Seminoles even farther south. The Treaty of Payne's Landing in 1832 called for Seminole removal to Indian Territory in Oklahoma. While the Seminoles fought hard in the Second Seminole War, from 1835 to 1842, some four thousand were forced to move west.

There were those, however, who remained. They farmed, hunted, and fished for their livelihood. They bought many of their goods in the American settlers' stores. They took part in the Green Corn Dance.

In Indian Territory, the Seminole Nation was formed in 1869. When the nation was dissolved in 1906, more than two thousand Seminoles were living in Oklahoma.

In Florida the Seminoles remained quite isolated until the opening of the Tamiami Trail in 1928. By 1941 many of Florida's Seminoles lived on three reservations; many lived on nonreservation lands. Those who lived along the Tamiami Trail organized as the Miccosukee Tribe in 1961.

Today there are more than a thousand Seminoles in Florida; at least 350 Miccosukee and perhaps 2,300 Seminoles are in Oklahoma. *See also* OSCEOLA.

**SEQUOYA** (1766–1839). The warrior-scribe of the Cherokee noted for putting together the Cherokee alphabet, or the "talking leaves." As a young man Sequoya was an able linguist. He learned French, Spanish, and English. But he was much opposed to the coming of Europeans and Americans to Cherokee country, what is now North Carolina, Georgia, and Tennessee. So, he moved west in 1797.

In 1821, after twelve years of work, Sequoya submitted his alphabet (ninety-two characters, later reduced to eighty-six) to the head men of the Cherokee, and they approved heartily. Cherokee of all ages began to learn to use the "talking leaves." Within a few months thousands were able to read and write in their own language. In 1824 parts of the Bible were printed in Cherokee. In 1828 the tribe published *The Cherokee Phoenix,* a weekly newspaper printed in both Cherokee and English.

**Sequoya**

In his later years Sequoya was active politically in Indian Territory. When many of the Cherokee moved west over the "Trail of Tears," it was Sequoya who helped to reunite them with their brothers. He visited many of the Indian tribes. He died while pursuing a lost band of Cherokee in the mountains of Tamaulipas in Mexico in 1839. *See also* CHEROKEE.

**SIOUX (DAKOTA).** Sioux beginnings can be traced to the Great Lakes, to Mille Lac, and to Lake of the Woods. There the Sioux built wigwams, harvested wild rice, planted maize, made maple sugar, and hunted deer. Pushed westward by the French fur traders and the Chippewa, the Sioux adapted to new environments. The Santee of Eastern Dakota remained close to their old haunts in Minnesota; the Yankton and Yanktonai of Middle Dakota moved to the edge of the prairie; the Teton of Western Dakota were the first of the Sioux to move to the Great Plains, where they became mounted horsemen, bison hunters, and extraordinary warriors.

The Teton roamed the Plains in small bands. Expert horsemen and marksmen, they brought the bison to earth with bow and arrow and gun. They called upon "medicine bundles" for spiritual power, and they danced the Sun Dance. They gained prestige in war by stealing horses. The women stripped the bison of skin and meat, prepared the pemmican, set up the tepees and took them down, packed the travoises, and cared for children and family.

When white Americans began to move west, the Sioux barred the way. In 1862 the Santee, under Little Crow, fell on the Minnesota settlements. Seven hundred civilians and a hundred soldiers were killed. The uprising was squelched, and the Santee were forced from their lands and moved to the Great Sioux Reservation in South Dakota. When gold was discovered in the Black Hills many more Americans moved into Sioux country. The army was ever present. On June 25, 1876, Sioux war parties under Sitting Bull, Crazy Horse, Spotted Tail, Red Cloud, and others cut up and destroyed the Seventh Cavalry under George A. Custer on the Little Bighorn. But the struggle was hardly over.

The bison were all but gone. There was little glory left for the Sioux hunters and warriors. In 1889 the Great Sioux Reservation was cut into smaller parts— Pine Ridge, Rosebud, and Standing Rock. In the same year the Ghost Dance reached the Sioux with its promise for a better life. The Sioux danced, and Americans were afraid. At Wounded Knee in 1890, jittery soldiers fired at and killed 200 Sioux in cold blood. The dead—men, women, and children—were buried in a common grave.

**Sioux women in festival clothing**

Life would change much for the Sioux during the twentieth century. There was schooling on and off the reservation, as well as loans for business enterprises and work with the Civilian Conservation Corps (CCC). During World War II there was military service, and after the war vocational training for veterans in the cities. But poor housing, poor health care, and inadequate water supplies remained. And on Pine Ridge in the early 1970s it was thought that the tribal chairman was in league with the BIA (Bureau of Indian Affairs).

The Sioux, supported by members of AIM (American Indian Movement), rebelled. In 1973 at Wounded Knee, they occupied the Catholic church and dug in to fight. Government forces also dug in. For seventy days the battle raged. Blood was shed, and Wounded Knee was left in shambles.

Today, ten years after the Second Battle of Wounded Knee, the Sioux reservations are relatively quiet, but the struggle for life and identity continues. *See also* AMERICAN INDIAN MOVEMENT; GHOST DANCE; *and* RED CLOUD.

**SITTING BULL** (1834–1890). A leading Sioux warrior–medicine man of the Hunkpapa Teton. At fourteen he had collected his first coups against the Crow. He took part in many of the Plains wars (1869–1876). It is said that he predicted, through a vision at a Sun Dance, the battle of the Little Bighorn in which General George A. Custer and the Seventh Cavalry were annihilated on June 25, 1876. Following the battle, the Teton medicine man led two thousand Sioux north to Canada—and freedom. Only hunger drove him to surrender, in 1881.

**Sitting Bull**

Sitting Bull was a prisoner at Fort Randall, South Dakota, until 1883. A man of quiet ways, a skillful organizer, a sacred dreamer, he stuck firmly to his Teton ideals. He could never be reconciled with the white settlers or their ways. He encouraged the first Ghost Dance on the Standing Rock Reservation. On December 15, 1890, Indian police, ordered to take him prisoner, shot him and his son Crow Foot to death.

**SQUAW.** The Narraganset term for woman. A similar term was also used by the Lenni-Lenape, Chippewa, and Cree. The term was carried widely across the United States and Canada by white explorers, traders, and settlers. It was adopted by many Indian tribes in the West.

**TAOS PUEBLO.** At the base of the Sangre de Cristo mountains, Taos Pueblo straddles both sides of the Taos River, seventy miles (112 km) northeast of Santa Fe, New Mexico. The Red Willow Place has been inhabited for more than six hundred years. The Taos were farmers of maize, squash, and beans and hunters of deer, elk, and bear in the mountains and antelope and rabbit in the nearby desert. They also gathered berries, nuts, and sage and fished for trout in lake and stream. Before the coming of the Spaniards they numbered about two thousand.

Coronado's lieutenants arrived in 1540 and 1541. They described the four- and five-story houses, the outside ladders, the seven kivas, and the planted fields. The later arrivals—civilian rulers, army officers and missionaries—came with heavy hands. Early in the seventeenth century the mission of San Geronimo was founded. The Taos were forced to abandon many of their old ways and convert to Catholicism. The Spanish language, horses and cattle, and new crops and farming techniques were also introduced to the Taos.

In 1680 the Taos revolted against the Spaniards in the Pueblo Revolt. They revolted again in 1693 and 1696, abandoning the pueblo. Finally forced to surrender, they returned to the Red Willow Place.

But the wars continued in the eighteenth century. The Taos built a defensive wall around the pueblo, but it did not deter the Ute, Comanche, and Apache raiders.

**Taos Pueblo**

In the nineteenth century there was a war with the Americans. The Taos hated the newly arrived American soldiers who stole their beef, their maize, and their women. Aroused by their Mexican neighbors, the Taos killed Governor Charles Bent and twenty other Americans. In retaliation the Americans killed fifteen Indian leaders.

Change has come rather slowly to conservative Taos. But additions have been made to the old buildings. There are windows and doors, as well as glass, in the lower stories of the pueblo. There are bicycles, cars, and trucks. There are fenced fields and flower beds. There is electricity, and gas and electrically operated appliances. There are six kivas. And there are fifteen hundred Indian people at or near Taos Pueblo today—a thousand who live on the reservation, five hundred who live elsewhere.

**TECUMSEH** (1768–1813). Tecumseh's message was clear. The Indians must return to a state of purity, they must no longer fight each other, and they must no longer sell Indian land to white settlers. Tecumseh, his brother the Shawnee Prophet, and their agents carried the message between the Dakotas and Florida.

When tribes in Indiana Territory sold their land to the United States in 1809, Tecumseh was furious. He protested to Governor William Henry Harrison, but nothing happened. In 1811 the governor moved troops to Prophet Town and destroyed it. But Tecumseh, too, was active. He carried his message to the southern tribes in 1811; he was ready for war.

Tecumseh joined the British as a brigadier general in the War of 1812. At the Battle of the Thames in Ontario in 1913, he shed his general's uniform, donned Indian deerskin, and was killed in front of his warriors.

**The death of Tecumseh**

**TEPEE (TIPI).** The portable dwelling of the tribes that moved from place to place. On the Great Plains the tepee was made over a frame of three or four poles on which as many as twenty others might be set. The poles were tied near the top with a hide rope. A bison covering made of fifteen to twenty skins was drawn around the pole frame. A skin door was added. Flaps, near the top, controlled the flow of the wind. On the Plains the woman was the tepee maker.

A fire pit was dug at the center. The smoke curled up and out of the smoke hole at the top. In hot weather the covers were raised to permit the air to flow through the tepee. In cold weather open spaces near the ground were lined with grass to keep the cold out.

The Crow probably made the finest tepees. Set over a four-pole frame, they stood 30 and 40 feet (9 and 12 m) high. They were beautifully painted and decorated. At a Crow camp circle as many as four hundred tepees could be seen in place at once.

**A Crow tepee**

**TOMAHAWK.** A favorite weapon of the Algonquian-speaking peoples of eastern North America. It looked much like a European hatchet. The stem and head were often made of solid wood. Occasionally spikes were inserted in the head. When going into battle, tribes painted the tomahawk red and then sent it to allied tribes who joined them at war. Tomahawks of a later time were made of metal or stone. They served as tools rather than weapons.

**The Trail of Tears**

**TRAIL OF TEARS.** The Treaty of New Echota of 1835 awarded the Cherokee seven million acres in northeastern Oklahoma, the Cherokee Strip, and in Kansas. But the Cherokee did not want to move. The United States government, committed to removal, sent Gen. Winfield Scott with seven thousand troops in 1838 to round up the dejected Cherokee.

John Ross, a Cherokee, urged that the "migration" be delayed until autumn. Many of his people, he said, would die on the march in the heat of summer. He suggested that the Cherokee themselves direct the move, and General Scott agreed. Organized in bands of about a thousand, under two able leaders, the Cherokee began to withdraw from their old haunts. On foot, in wagons, and on horseback, thirteen thousand men, women, and children moved into Tennessee and Kentucky. They crossed the Ohio and Mississippi rivers. On March 26, 1839, the last of their number arrived in Indian Territory. But four thousand had died on the "Trail of Tears" from the miseries and hardships of the journey. *See also* CHEROKEE *and* JOHN ROSS.

# U-V

**UTE.** Home for the Ute was amid the mountains and valleys of central and western Colorado, eastern Utah, and northern New Mexico. Gatherers of roots and wild seeds and hunters of antelope and rabbit, the Ute also became raiders after they acquired the horse from the Spaniards in the seventeenth century. Their war parties attacked the Rio Grande Pueblos. Mounted on horseback, the Ute hunted the bison on the Great Plains in the eighteenth century.

In the nineteenth century American explorers, miners, and settlers began to move into Ute territory. The first treaty was signed in 1849. In 1861 the Uinta band was confined to the Uinta Valley; in 1863 a reservation was set aside for the Tabeguache band. Americans continued to whittle away at the Ute land base. The Ute numbered about four thousand in 1870.

In 1879 the Yampa and White River bands turned on Indian agent Nathan Meeker, who wanted the Ute to become farmers, and the whites. The agency buildings were burned, and Meeker was killed. An army under Maj. T.T. Thornburgh was ambushed; fourteen of the major's soldiers were slaughtered. Finally, a large federal and state force drove the Ute onto a new reservation in Utah.

The Ute were impoverished. Under their chiefs, Ouray and Buckskin Charlie, they attempted to conform to the white settlers' ways. They sent their young people to school; they tried to farm the harsh Utah earth. Many left the reservation and took up the old Ute life-style—living in the karnee and gathering roots and wild seeds. They danced the Bear Dance and borrowed the Sun Dance from the Plains Indians.

Conditions did not improve until the 1950s. In 1950 the Confederated Ute Tribes won their case in the United States Court of Claims claiming they had been defrauded of their land in the nineteenth century. The confederated tribes were awarded $31 million. Oil and natural gas discoveries also yielded a considerable amount of money. The newfound wealth was spent on housing, electricity, telephones, and water. It was spent on irrigation, professional training, livestock, timber enterprises, health purposes, and the development of tourism.

In 1968 the Confederated Ute Tribes beame the Ute Mountain Agency (most of it is in southwestern Colorado) and the Southern Ute Agency (southwestern Colorado), respectively. Both are continuing their development. The Northern Ute live on the Uinta and Ouray reservations. Today the combined Ute number about four thousand.

**Ute on
the warpath**

**VISION QUEST.** On the Great Plains, warriors preparing for battle and young men reaching puberty sought supernatural power through a vision quest. They took sweatbaths to make themselves clean and pure. They went for days without food; they prayed and mutilated their bodies. The Crow were known to chop the joint from a forefinger and offer it to the rising sun. They might slit their chests or backs, insert thongs, tie themselves to poles or bison skulls, and then run until their flesh was pried loose. The greater the agony, the more possible a vision.

The vision itself often came in the form of an animal, a bird, or an insect, the earth, moon, or stars. Each would serve as a guardian spirit. A sacred song might accompany the vision. So might the symbols of the warrior's newfound power—feathers, skins, stones, and bones. These were placed in the so-called medicine bundle. They made up the medicine, or the power.

It was not only the warrior or the young man reaching puberty who sought a vision. When faced with hunger, disease, and the other calamities of life, the men of the Great Plains and other areas sought a vision in the hope of finding a guardian spirit who would help them through their personal ordeals.

**WICKIUP.** The name given by whites to the brush shelter or mat-covered dwelling of the Paiute and the Apache. The Paiute, however, used the term *karnee* for their dwelling. *See also* KARNEE.

**WIGWAM.** The dwelling of many Algonquian-speaking peoples from Canada to North Carolina. Materials used in construction varied, often depending upon plant materials that were available.

The Chippewa put a number of poles or saplings in place in an oval or circle, bent them over and tied them together with basswood bark. They strengthened the dwelling by tying other saplings crosswise between the poles. They lashed bulrush mats over the frame and covered the roof with birch bark. Chippewa farther north used birch bark and the bark of the black ash to make the wigwam.

The Micmac of Nova Scotia made small circular birch bark wigwams large enough for a single family. When available, skins, mats, or green boughs were used for covers, and the covers could be moved from place to place. In more recent times the wigwams were covered with tar paper.

**SARAH WINNEMUCCA** (1844–1891). An early Paiute battler for Indian rights and justice. She was a daughter of Chief Winnemucca, whose band ranged widely between Honey Lake in California, Pyramid Lake in Nevada, and the Humboldt Sink. She grew up in the Paiute lifeway.

At age sixteen Sarah accompanied her grandfather, Chief Truckee, on a visit to California. She remained there to live with a white family and attend school. She learned to speak English quite well.

Meanwhile, white settlers were moving across the Nevada desert and through Paiute country. Many battles were fought. Many Paiute were killed, including Sarah's mother, brother, and a sister. The survivors were moved to the reservation, officially proclaimed in 1874, near Pyramid Lake.

Paiute were also sent to the Malheur Reservation in Oregon in 1872. Sarah became an interpreter there. She also taught at the local school. During the Bannock War in 1878 she offered her services to the army as peacemaker. In a dash into Bannock country she persuaded her father, Chief Winnemucca, to give up the fight.

When Paiute were sent to the Yakima Reservation in the state of Washington, Chief Winnemucca and Sarah went to Washington, D.C., to argue the Paiute case in 1879 and 1880. President Rutherford B. Hayes and Secretary of Interior Carl Schurz both agreed that the Paiute should return to the Malheur Reservation. But the order for the return was never made by the Indian agent at Yakima. A number of the Paiute merely drifted south.

Sarah, aroused by the hostility of the Indian agents, went on a lecture tour in the East. She wanted justice for the Paiute. And she got much sympathy. Her book, *Life Among the Paiutes,* was published in 1884.

Sarah Winnemucca, tired and mentally ill, retired to a sister's home in Montana. She died there on October 16, 1891. *See also* PAIUTE.

**YAQUI.** The Rio Yaqui empties into the Gulf of California in Mexico's north-western state of Sonora. Yaqui *rancherias* or settlements—eighty in number in the seventeenth century—lined both sides of the river. Homes were either dome-shaped and mat-covered or rectangular with flat roofs; they were made from cane or wattle and daub.

The river valley environment was a rich one. The Yaqui were farmers of maize, squash, beans, and cotton; gatherers of mesquite pods, roots, and wild fruits; hunters, primarily of deer; and fishermen. They lived well. Each rancheria was an independent unit. But in time of trouble the Yaqui could muster six thousand warriors!

In 1609 the Spaniards invaded the Yaqui country but were driven back. The Jesuits arrived in 1617 and by 1619 had baptized nearly all of the Yaqui. They reduced the eighty rancherias to eight towns, each with a plaza, an adobe church, and a mission house. Beyond stretched the corrals and the fenced fields. The Yaqui were introduced to the Spanish language, to the art of writing, to the six-day workweek, and to a host of Catholic ceremonials.

In 1740 the Yaqui revolted, not against the Jesuits, but against the Spanish civil government and the Spanish military. At the Hill of Bones the Yaqui lost five thousand of their people.

There were other outbreaks. When Mexico became an independent state in 1821 the government attempted to dominate the Indian tribes, to tax them, and to have the young men serve in the Mexican armed forces. Again the Yaqui rebelled. Juan Banderas, who wanted to set up an independent Indian state, led the Yaqui, Pima, Opata, and Mayo into battle. They were badly beaten by the Mexican army in 1833.

The Yaqui attempted to regroup. They reorganized Eight Towns, they reworked the *pascola* arts or costumed dances, and they organized their own cavalry and infantry units, but to no avail. The Mexican armies came down upon them. Many Yaqui fled—to distant mines, haciendas, and fishing villages, and to the urban areas. In the 1870s the Yaqui numbered about nine thousand.

The worst, however, was yet to come. In 1903 the Mexican government began to deport the Yaqui. More than five thousand were sold for sixty pesos each and sent as slaves to the Yucatan and Oaxaca. The tales of brutality from that experience still circulate in the Yaqui villages. The Yaqui also began to move to Arizona and the barrios on the edges of Phoenix and Tucson.

In 1939 the Mexican government set land aside for the Yaqui on the north bank of Rio Yaqui. Yaqui were encouraged to return to the motherland. Some did. Many did not. The Yaqui who chose to remain in Arizona have been greatly influenced by the American experience; they have retained, however, a strong Yaqui identity. The Yaqui who make their homes on or near Rio Yaqui have adapted well to the Mexican experience. In Mexico and the United States the Yaqui number well over ten thousand today.

# Z

**ZUNI.** The Zuni believe that their pueblo, in all-too-dry New Mexico, is the middle place—*itiwana*—or center of the world. The world is one. And everyone and everything in it is alive and must be kept in harmony. That can only happen, the Zuni believe, through prayer and by participating in the proper rituals or ceremonies. In the summer the Zuni urge the gods to bring rain and rich harvests; in the winter they are concerned with fertility, medicine, and war. They call upon the Sun Priest to protect the pueblo; they call upon their ancestors, the "rainmakers," and kachinas to bring water to the fields. There are ceremonies for the War Gods, the Bow Priests, and the Beast Gods. At the winter solstice the Shalako, wearing giant wooden masks, enter the pueblo and offer prayers for prosperity, fertility, long life, and happiness.

Spaniards, seeking the Seven Cities of Cibola, saw the Zuni for the first time in 1539. Coronado stormed one of the pueblos (there were probably six or seven at the time) in 1540, as the Zuni took refuge on nearby Taaiyalone Mountain. When the Zuni killed the Franciscan missionaries who had been sent among them in 1632, they again retired to the mountain. They also went to the mountain at the time of the Pueblo Revolt in 1680 and again in 1703 after the killing of the mission priest.

Through all of their difficulties the Zuni men continued to plant and harvest maize, squash, and beans. They hunted the rabbit. In their small gardens the

**A Zuni
rain dance**

Zuni women grew tomatoes, onions, and chili peppers. They gathered wild fruits, seeds, and piñon nuts. And the old religious ceremonies continued to be performed.

Today there is a single pueblo at the old site on the Zuni Reservation with a population of about six thousand. The homes, on single lots, are flat topped and made of quarried stones or cement blocks. They support TV aerials. There are cars and trucks, electric power, and a modern water supply. There are the small farming communities: Tekapo, Pescado, Nutria, and Ojo Caliente. There are elementary schools and a high school. Since 1970 the Zuni have been in charge of the programs that were set up by the BIA. And, as in bygone days, the Shalako continued to perform at the time of the winter solstice.

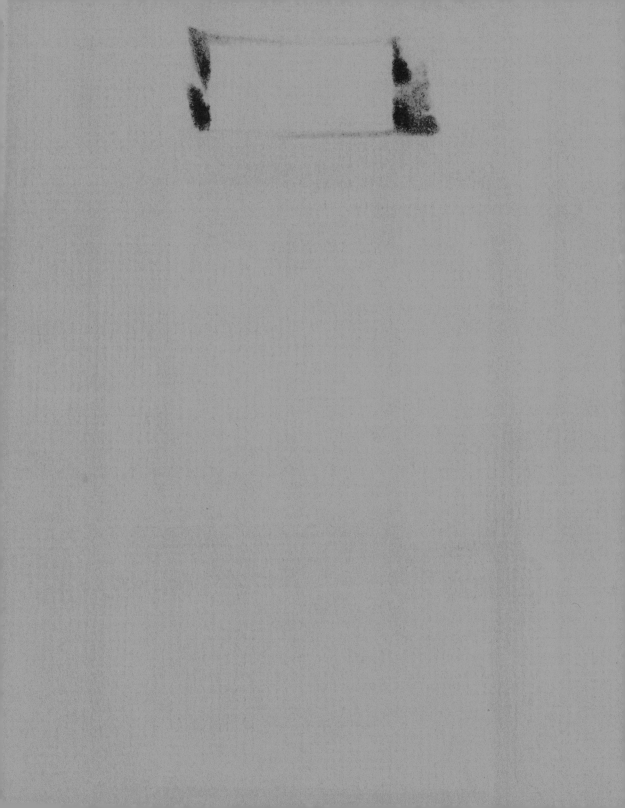